This book offers a wonderfully practical look at how people move from a relationship in which God is unknown to one in which he is fully known. Through life experiences, ministry testimonies, and biblical engagement, Dr. Luchetti encourages you to go deep spiritually along with those around you. Dr. Luchetti provides a framework for discipleship that is memorable and transferrable—a helpful guide for pastors and ministry leaders.

—COLLEEN DERR, associate professor, Congregational Spiritual Formation and Christian Ministries, Wesley Seminary

True Depth is a vital book for this day. This book has depth but is understandable and moves beyond Western "churchanity" to biblical Christianity. I believe the use of this book will be a catalyst in any congregation to new depths and transformation of churches and communities thoughout the nation.

—JO ANNE LYON, General Superintendent of The Wesleyan Church

This book will both encourage your heart and challenge your thinking. It inspires and instructs toward three huge ideas: God is the primary maker of deep disciples; the church, though flawed, is the beautiful environment God designed to support disciple-making; and Christians can live a more vibrant and deeper life in Christ! *True Depth* is theological and practical, filled with honest stories that will grab your heart. If you'd like to see discipleship become more spiritually organic and less culturally organized, this book is for you.

—DAN REILAND, executive pastor of 12Stone Church

This book powerfully unfolds how God develops deep disciples in Christian community.

—WAYNE SCHMIDT, vice president of Wesley Seminary

With clear language, Lenny Luchetti unpacks what's involved in growing into maturity in the faith. As with most things of God there's more going on than initially m
us see what we'd otherwise miss.

—MARSHALL

Revelation. Restoration. Transformation. Sanctification. Mission. With these five words, Lenny Luchetti gives us not only a biblical vision, but a theological mission with a practical outline. *True Depth* is a tour de force into the Wesleyan way of "practical divinity."

—J. D. WALT, Seedbed's sower-in-chief

This book is filled with the same forward-thinking spirit that defines its author. Lenny Luchetti's challenge is classically timeless, but everything about the way he writes and thinks feels fresh. For those who are jaded by the church or have become cynical about the lack of true disciples in our time, *True Depth* presents a hopeful way forward.

—DARREN WHITEHEAD, pastor and author of *Rumors of God*

This is not another trendy book on discipleship, but a genuine, clear approach with practical exercises that will help church attendees dive deeply into Christlike living. First it will change you, and then it will change your church.

—BOB WHITESEL, award-winning author of *The Healthy Church* and *Cure for the Common Church*

TRUE DEPTH

MOVING BEYOND CULTURAL CHURCHIANITY

Lenny Luchetti

wesleyan
PUBLISHING HOUSE
wphstore.com

Copyright © 2015 by Lenny Luchetti
Published by Wesleyan Publishing House
Indianapolis, Indiana 46250
Printed in the United States of America
ISBN: 978-0-89827-980-1
ISBN (e-book): 978-0-89827-981-8

Library of Congress Cataloging-in-Publication Data

Luchetti, Lenny.
   True depth : moving beyond cultural churchianity / Lenny Luchetti.
       pages cm
   Includes bibliographical references.
   ISBN 978-0-89827-980-1 (pbk.)
   1. Spiritual formation. I. Title.
   BV4511.L83 2015
   269--dc23
                                          2015009223

To the people of the two churches whose testimonies pepper these pages. Stroudsburg Wesleyan Church and College Wesleyan Church showed me what it looks like to swim in the deep end of the discipleship pool.

CONTENTS

For free shepherding resources,
visit wphresources.com/truedepth.

ACKNOWLEDGEMENTS

Several times during the writing of this book I felt as if I were floundering in water over my head. Thankfully, I have friends who helped me stay afloat. These swimming partners offered valuable critique to improve what I originally submitted to them. They were kind enough to affirm the book's strengths too. I solicited their aid not only because of their observant reader's eye or insightful writer's hand, but also because they are disciples of true depth.

Some heroes on my swim team are Elaine Bernius, Keith Drury, Nate Foster, Bif Fry, Scott Hughes, Matthew Johnson, Amy Luchetti, Laurel Roberts, Erica Sallo, and Ken Schenck. Many of the insights you may glean from *True Depth* can be attributed, no doubt, to their input.

Others on my swim team increased the value of *True Depth*. Their testimonies are splattered throughout these pages. I received dozens of testimonies from disciples at College Wesleyan Church and Stroudsburg Wesleyan Church. Every one of their stories inspired me, but I could include only a few in *True Depth* to inspire you.

The team at Wesleyan Publishing House is distinct in their ability to help writers swim in deep waters. My gratitude especially extends to Kevin Scott, who pushed me into the pool of this project, and to Craig Bubeck, who assisted me in completing my swim.

God keeps figuring out how to make disciples of true depth. Then he finds ways for them to surround me. Whenever I find myself playing it safe in the shallow waters or venturing in over my head in the depths, God throws me a life preserver called the church. Long before I could even articulate the discipleship dynamics presented in this book, I witnessed people of depth living them. My life and this book are better because of it.

INTRODUCTION
SWIMMING IN THE DEEP END

The sixth year of Sam's life was defining. His fear of taking a risk kept him from venturing into the deep end of our community pool. As a dad, I wanted him to be generally averse to risk. But this was different. He was a good swimmer, completely capable of thriving in water over his head. I tried to coax him into the deep end numerous times. "Come on, Sam, you can do it!" I even resorted to bribery: "If you jump into the deep end, I will take you out for ice cream, let you watch your favorite movie, and allow you to stay up late tonight." He didn't budge. I whispered threats: "Sam, if you don't jump into the deep end of the pool right now, no ice cream, no movie, and no staying up late." Clearly, this is not a book on how to parent.

My bribes and threats didn't inspire Sam to do what I knew he could do. He'd had swimming lessons and lots of practice. He was physically ready to launch out of the shallow end of the pool into the depths with his older brother and sister. But was he ready internally? In order to go boldly where he had not gone before, Sam had to become discontent with shallow-water walking and be willing to overcome his fear of deep-water swimming.

One day it happened. Sam became so bored in the shallows that he was willing to risk a jump into the six-foot abyss. When he did, the joy on his face and in his voice was priceless. "Daddy, I'm swimming in the deep end! Look at me, Daddy. I knew I could do it. Are you proud of me, Daddy? Can I have ice cream? Can I watch a movie? Can I stay up late? Please, Daddy? You said I could."

"Absolutely, Sam!" My son seemed to grow a foot taller that day. His willingness to forsake status quo and take a risk matured him.

God is calling his kids out of the boredom of shallow discipleship and into the adventure of deep discipleship. We don't need to rely on a floatation device. Our heavenly Father has taught us how to swim. We were made for the depths of a discipleship journey worth living and dying for.

YOUR SWIM COACH

Christians are bored with the trite and trendy. The church needs another trendy discipleship book as much as it needs more announcements during the Sunday worship service. We don't want another book that takes the reader's soul on a long bus ride only to drop it off exactly where it was picked up. Too many discipleship resources focus on what *we* can do to make disciples. This book emphasizes what *God* does to make disciples through the local church.

Disciples are starving for the significance and stretching that comes with a radical and risky relationship with Christ. We hunger for substance not safety and status quo. I offer *True Depth* as a faithful response to the hunger pains of twenty-first-century Christians.

Here are a few noteworthy features of this book:

- Reflection questions to guide individuals and groups in exploring the dynamics of deep discipleship.
- Practical exercises that are congruent with the life Christ lived and calls us to embrace.
- Testimonial excerpts from disciples like you who are seeking to swim in the depths.

Deep disciples are not self-made but God-made. They are formed by revelation (what God does *among* us), restoration (what God does *for* us), transformation (what God does *to* us), sanctification (what God does *in* us), and mission (what God does *through* us). These five discipleship dynamics provide a paradigm for true depth, and they form the core chapters of this book. The sequencing of the chapters does not suggest a step-by-step progression. For deep-end disciples, these five dynamics happen always and everywhere, simultaneously and continuously.

Too many Christians are experiencing a bland brand of discipleship that feels more burdensome than liberating. *True Depth* is written for Christians who want to experience an authentic and adventurous discipleship swim. This book is also written for pastors and small-group leaders who want to help people grow in Christ so they can swim in the deep end. The discipleship dynamics presented here are accessible and adaptable to a broad range of Christians and denominations.

SWIMMER'S PRAYER

God, if you are with us, nothing else matters. And if you are not with us, nothing else matters. Be with us. We submit ourselves to your revelation, restoration, transformation, sanctification, and mission. Do something among, for, to, in, and through us. We pray these things only and always for your glory and for the good of the world you created, sustain, and love. Amen!

CULTURAL CHURCHIANITY VERSUS BIBLICAL CHRISTIANITY

1

Swimming in the shallows has caused the church to sink. It's easy to find statistics, polls, and trends that expose current discipleship challenges. God has called disciples out of darkness and into light, out of the world and into Christ. Yet differences between Christians and non-Christians are difficult to detect. The divorce rates, addiction patterns, spending habits, and leisure activities for those inside the church are surprisingly similar to those outside the church. Evidently, Christians are not making much of a splash in the shallows.

Part of the problem is that people have been immunized against biblical Christianity. Certain high-profile preachers and the electronic and print media that propagate their messages are the primary culprits. These teachers lead people to believe that following Christ cultivates a cozy, comfortable, and convenient sort of life. The susceptible masses assume that, in Christ, every day is a Friday. But more often the actual discipleship journey feels like a Monday. A cozy inner tube is not available when swimming in the depths with Christ. There's only a cross with a cost.

The American dream has hijacked Christian discipleship. Simply put, the gospel of health, wealth, and happiness has produced a church, primarily in North America, in which disciples are just treading shallow water. That's the bad news. The good news is that many of these disciples are starving, nearly to spiritual death, for something more significant.

The Christian gospel includes both connection and confrontation. The challenge is in trying to discern which core elements of the gospel connect to the culture and which ones confront the culture. In too many instances, the church's historic and current attempts to connect the gospel to culture compromised and even contradicted the gospel. Like oil and water, peanut butter and Italian dressing, and an orange shirt and red pants, some things just don't blend. Cultural "churchianity," built on personal preferences, narcissistic consumerism, rugged individualism, and safe status quo, absolutely cannot mix with biblical Christianity. Biblical Christianity involves cross bearing, self-denial, and costly sacrificial love.

A "churchian," not to be mistaken for a Christian, swims in the shallows. A churchian attends church gatherings, serves others, and seems moral. He is a good person. He practices spiritual disciplines but usually only when he wants something from God. He tries to be generous. He looks a lot like a true disciple. However, *he* is the center of his religion. He keeps Christ at arm's length. He follows what he perceives to be God's will as long as it aligns with his conception of "the good life."

> *I assumed the safe answer was the right answer. Jesus never called us to be safe!*
> —Michelle

As soon as Christ makes demands, as he often does, problems arise. The churchian ignores any call to deny self and pick up the cross. The cross and cost do not figure into his religion of comfort and convenience.

Although we cannot assume that people become deep disciples simply because they attend church, disciples are not made without the church. Disciples will never learn to swim in the depths without the help of a local church community. God is the one who makes disciples, but he does so through the church. Disciples of depth cannot be made outside of the context of Christian community.

A HAUNTING QUESTION

Some questions challenge and, at times, haunt every generation of Christians. One of the big questions standing nose to nose with the church today is, "Are disciples actually being made?" I heard Jim Herrington, a former Southern Baptist pastor who resides in Houston, Texas, wrestle with this question. I visited Houston as part of my doctoral studies to explore the many different sizes and styles of churches that exist in that city. I visited black, white, and multi-ethnic churches that were large, mid-size, and small. They ranged from traditional, contemporary, and emergent in urban, rural, or suburban settings. What stood out to me most from that field trip was Jim's question. It haunted me.

"Are disciples really being made?" Jim asked. He had resigned as pastor of a megachurch because he believed too much distance had come between him and the people he was called to disciple. He admitted being too busy programming the church to find time to disciple the people. So Jim purchased a home in Montrose, a red-light district of Houston. He opened his home to runaways, prostitutes, addicts, alcoholics, transvestites, and whoever was homeless and hungry for hope. Jim welcomed this assorted crew and finally felt he was close enough to people to partner with God in making disciples. As far as I could tell from the stories he told, God was transforming lives. People on the fringe were not only coming to faith in Christ, but also learning to swim in the deep end of the discipleship pool.

It is possible for any church to make disciples. An unfair assumption is that large churches don't make disciples, while small churches do. The fact is some megachurches hit the ball out of the park when it comes to forming biblical Christians. I also know of small churches that are better at forming cultural churchians than they are at making disciples. A church's size does not matter.

During that trip to Houston, I met another pastor who had resigned from traditional local church ministry. He had purchased a bar as an outreach to people far from God. I met with him to learn from his strategy for evangelism and discipleship. His evangelistic plan was simple. He hosted Friday night poker at the bar. Texas hold 'em, no doubt.

He seemed to have a strong intent to reach out and build bridges to people. "But what are you doing to disciple the people God brings your way?" I inquired. His discipleship plan was even simpler. It was nonexistent, really. "I don't have a plan for that," he admitted unapologetically. I wonder how many local churches have, figuratively speaking, purchased a bar to reach people without a plan to grow them.

I, too, was guilty of putting most, if not all, of my eggs in the outreach basket. Somehow I had forgotten that the best way to evangelize sinners is to disciple saints. When disciples of true depth embody the Christ-life among family members, friends, and coworkers, the evangelistic sparks fly. I knew this fact, but somehow I had managed to ignore it consistently.

The congregation I most recently served as pastor had a solid plan for reaching people who were disconnected from intimate relationship with God. This is partly why the congregation nearly tripled in size in six years. Hundreds of people crossed the line of faith in Christ, and many of them were baptized. Baptism formed the backbone of our discipleship process. In fact, it was pretty much the extent of our discipleship plan. Sure, we invited people to grow through small groups and service opportunities, but in a soft-sell kind of way. We didn't want to scare away the new people who were coming into the life of our church. This was a bad strategy. I thought we were doing great. We weren't. My failure to initiate a biblical and intentional discipleship plan allowed new Christians to swim in the shallow end of the pool for far too long. Like my son Sam, many of these new disciples were completely capable of swimming in the deep end, but I didn't encourage or teach them how. I was better at making churchians than Christians. According to national statistics and expert analysis, our congregation was more the norm than the exception. How, then, do we move out of the shallows and into the depths where we are in over our heads, caught up in the discipleship adventure of a lifetime?

ONCE UPON A TIME . . .

In a faraway place, long, long ago, a group of people began to follow Jesus. His life and teaching captivated them. He drew them into discipleship, a journey of learning, praying, growing, going, giving, and serving. Into their lives flowed meaning, forgiveness, joy, purpose, peace, and love like they had never known. But unexpected ridicule, persecution, and pain also flooded their lives. Some of these disciples began to stall. They began to wonder if following Jesus was worth the cost. If they continued to stay on the discipleship journey, they would end up in water over their heads. These first-century followers floated in the middle of the pool trying to decide whether to choose the safe shallows or the risky depths. They realized there was no discount on the cost of discipleship.

Mark wrote his gospel to encourage these indecisive disciples to reach forward and kick toward the deep end. Rome's intense persecution of Christians in the first century made venturing into true depth extremely costly. It was tempting for disciples to choose the shallows. They could easily dog paddle toward them by compromising Christian convictions and accepting some of the pagan practices of Rome. Some did.

Mark's gospel inspired some deliberating disciples to swim from inch-deep dedication to mile-deep devotion. How did Mark do this? He concluded that the best way was to show them Jesus. The punch line of Mark's gospel is, "If you want to know what discipleship looks like, focus on Jesus, not the disciples." All four gospels highlight how clueless those first followers were, but Mark's gospel is especially brutal in its depiction of Peter, James, John, and the rest of the crew.

Cultural churchianity framed my view of Christianity in my early years. If my discipleship journey did not look like what churchianity dictated, I thought I was doing something wrong. In short, cultural churchianity limited my freedom in Christ. How sad. This trend not only stifled me, but it also grieved the Father.

—Laura

Mark offers a daring and life-altering vision of discipleship. Disciples in the twenty-first century need this message at least as much as, and maybe even more than, those in first-century Rome, who were struggling to swim. Many of us have discovered that while following Jesus certainly has its perks, the cost makes the superficial shallow end look more attractive than it is. The stakes are high, and the sacrifices are significant in the deep end. Mark refused to diminish the cost of the cross for Christ-followers. His gospel, then, serves as an insightful basis for the discipleship dynamics presented in this book.

TIME TO LAUNCH

Be warned. As you read on, you will encounter questions designed to have a hauntingly holy influence upon you: Is my life marked more by cultural churchianity than biblical Christianity? Do I love God better as I grow older? Am I playing life safe in the shallows or venturing out deeper into the discipleship pool? Do I resist the urge to build my kingdom so that I can focus the best of my resources on building God's kingdom? Has my willingness to deny myself, take up my cross, and follow Jesus decreased or increased over time? Is my relationship with Christ stagnant or growing? Am I really a disciple?

Swimming in the shallows will cause the church to sink. It's time for followers of Christ to launch out into the depths. God is not looking for churchians, but for Christians. The Holy Spirit, through the local church, equips and empowers us to swim in the deep end of the discipleship pool. God gives us arms to reach and legs to kick so that we can not merely survive, but thrive in the depths. When we dare to launch out to where "deep calls to deep" (Ps. 42:7), we find the faithful, fruitful, and fulfilling waters for which we thirst. Are you ready for true depth?

SWIMMING PRINCIPLE

God makes disciples through the church, when they swim away from the shallows of cultural churchianity and toward the depths of biblical Christianity.

SWIMMING PRACTICE

What do you think are the differences between cultural churchianity and biblical Christianity?

How does your life and local church reflect the values of either shallow churchianity or deep Christianity?

Where are you swimming in the discipleship pool? Are you in the shallows, in the deep, or in the middle and deciding where to swim? Where would those who know you best plot your location in the discipleship pool?

What decisions will you make today in order to launch deeper into the discipleship pool?

SWIMMER'S PRAYER

Lord, forgive us for swimming at times in the safe shallow pool, barely making a splash in our commitment to you. Thank you for empowering us with the spiritual arms and legs we need to thrive in the deep end with Christ. Give us the audacity to do whatever it takes to launch into the depths of discipleship. Amen.

REVELATION

WHAT GOD DOES AMONG US

2

Have you played hide-and-seek with a toddler? A toddler is terrible at the game. She wants to be found, and fast. You send the kid off to hide, hoping to sneak in a few more sips of coffee or finish cleaning the breakfast mess. Not gonna happen. After thirty seconds or so of hiding, the hyperactive toddler will giggle and yell repeatedly, "Come find me." The voice gives away her location. But, just to be sure you can find her, she screams out, "I'm in the bathroom." You ignore her cry to be found so you can continue to drink your coffee or do your chores. If you wait too long to find her, she will come out of hiding to find you. She wants to be found. She hates to be hidden.

God doesn't want to be hidden. He wants to be found. This is the picture of God painted by Mark's gospel.

We learn from Mark that Jesus tried to keep his messianic identity a secret at times (see 1:43–45; 8:29–30). However, a close reading of Mark also reveals a God who wants to be found. God kept showing up and speaking to humanity to reveal Jesus Christ's identity and mission. When he did, some got it. Some didn't.

JESUS GOT IT

God the Father showed up to speak to Jesus. In Mark 1:9–11, he revealed Jesus' identity in dramatic fashion. Jesus went to the Jordan River to be baptized by John. We read that heaven was "torn open" and that the Spirit descended on Jesus. Then "a voice came from heaven," the voice of God the Father, and spoke a revelatory word directly to Jesus. He said, "You are my Son, whom I love; with you I am well pleased" (v. 11).

God showed up to speak a word of revelation regarding Jesus' identity. As Mark's gospel unfolds, it becomes clear that Jesus embraced this revelation. He affirmed himself as the divine and beloved Son of God. The occasion of this revelation of his identity to the world changed everything for Jesus. His mission was clear. Jesus was fully human, just like us. He was, then, just as dependent upon God for revelation as we are. Jesus had his identity and mission revealed to him from someplace beyond himself. Jesus was always God, but when "he made himself nothing" (Phil. 2:7), he set aside his power, privilege, and position. He likely realized his identity mainly through the Spirit's revelation.

Jesus' life teaches us that to be fully human is to deeply depend upon God for identity-shaping, mission-directing revelation. God tore open the heavens to provide a revelation for Jesus. God will find a way to break the barrier that blocks his revelation. It's as if God is crying out, "Here I am! Come find me!"

THE DISCIPLES MISSED IT

Whenever God showed up to speak up in the gospel of Mark, Jesus got it. The disciples, however, typically missed it. Throughout Mark, the disciples were quite clueless about Jesus' identity and mission, but the account of Jesus' transfiguration makes this fact especially clear (see Mark 9:2–7).

Here, God was at it again. This time he revealed Jesus' identity and authority with miraculous dramatic flair. God went over the top because the disciples were rather dense. He brought Moses, the lawgiver, and Elijah, the prophet, to the mountain with Jesus. (Moses and Elijah had been dead for hundreds of years.) As they met, Jesus' clothes became a dazzling white. Peter, James, and John, the apostolic cream of the crop, were with Jesus. They might have wondered if someone had slipped a psychedelic drug in their matzo ball soup. God showed up and spoke up to reveal Jesus' identity to the disciples. He thundered: "This is my Son, whom I love. Listen to him!" (v. 7).

The disciples still didn't get it. This weighty revelation went right over Peter's head. We know this because he wanted to build not one but three tabernacles. Possibly he thought Jesus was merely on par with Moses (a representative of the Law) and Elijah (a representative of the Prophets). But the whole point of the revelation was that Jesus supersedes the Law and the Prophets.

Or maybe the disciples sought to erect tabernacles as a base from which Jesus could establish a glorious political kingdom on earth. They wanted the oppressive Romans gone and the Jews back on top of the world again. The disciples, we see, had selective hearing. They forgot what Jesus had told them back in Mark 8:31—that being the Messiah would entail suffering and shame, not power and prosperity.

Even with a dramatic mountaintop revelation like this one, which included heroic dead guys like Moses and Elijah, the disciples still didn't understand. How could these disciples, who were nearly always in close proximity to Jesus, miss revelation almost every time? If Peter, James, and John—Jesus' inner circle—could miss it, anyone can.

THE RELIGIOUS LEADERS RESISTED IT

Even a casual reading of Mark's gospel highlights a God who was and is chomping at the bit to be found. He kept showing up and speaking up to reveal Jesus' mission and identity not only to Jesus, but also to almost everyone else.

In Mark 14:61–65, God was at it again. Jesus was never more overtly self-revealing than he was with the high priest. Jesus was on trial before the Jewish ruling council called the Sanhedrin. The high priest asked Jesus bluntly, "Are you the Messiah?" (v. 61). Jesus, who up to this point in the trial had been secretive about his identity, responded, "I am" (v. 62). Revelation generally doesn't come more neatly packaged than that. The high priest, however, defiantly resisted this revelation of the Messiah, the one he was supposed to have been waiting for his entire life.

The high priest refused to let God tear open a new revelation. Why did he resist the Messiah? Because the revelation was like a pill he could not or would not swallow. The pill defied the high priest's theological expectations and religious traditions. The Jewish leaders blindfolded Jesus but, ironically, they were the ones who were blind to God's ultimate self-revelation. God himself stood in front of them and plainly said, "I am the Messiah! Here I am. Come find me."

28   The Jewish Sanhedrin was full of religious people. They were steeped in the Scriptures from birth. They fasted and prayed often. They worshiped in the temple daily. They observed the Sabbath and feasts. They waited and watched for the Messiah. Yet when the Messiah showed up to speak up, they defiantly resisted him.

Their ignorance is laughable. The comedy becomes tragedy, however, when we realize that their resistance to revelation put them in a spiritual cell and Jesus on a shameful cross. The comedy turns to further tragedy when we recognize that if well-informed religious people could resist a significant and explicit revelation from God, any of us can.

A CENTURION GOT IT

As we journey through Mark's gospel, we encounter a self-revealing God who kept showing up and speaking up because he wanted to be found. The disciples cluelessly missed the revelation, and the religious leaders defiantly resisted it. The only ones who really knew Jesus' identity were Jesus and demons. Near the very end of the gospel, though, we meet someone else who received a revelation of who Jesus is. God once again tore something open to reveal Jesus' identity. This time the curtain of the temple "was torn in two from top to bottom," as Jesus died on the cross (Mark 15:38).

Mark created bookends, coming full circle to end where he began. In chapter 1, God tore something open (the heavens) to reveal the identity of Jesus to Jesus. And Jesus got it. Then in chapter 15, God tore something open again (the temple curtain) to reveal the identity of Jesus to a most unlikely character—a Roman centurion. The centurion professed, "Surely this man was the Son of God" (v. 39). The centurion got it.

The handpicked disciples didn't always get revelation when it came to them. The high priest and other religious leaders resisted it.

29

Yet this non-Jewish, Roman centurion employed by evil Caesar embraced the revelation.

It is doubtful that the centurion was waiting for the Messiah. He was probably not familiar with the Scriptures. He probably did not worship in the temple. But when God showed up to speak up, this theologically unsophisticated centurion got it.

It's possible to be immersed in religion, as the high priest was, and yet resist God's revelation. It's possible to be in close proximity to Jesus, as the apostles were, and still miss God's revelation. It's possible, then, for you and me to resist or miss an identity-shaping, mission-directing revelation from God when he shows up to speak up.

Like a child desperate to be found, God still reveals himself to humanity. He is actively tearing apart the heavens and ripping the curtain so he can reveal himself and his will to us. God will break through the barriers that block his revelation. When he does, will we miss, resist, or embrace the revelation?

THE CHURCH'S FOUNDATION IS REVELATION

Eventually, those early disciples became receptive to identity-shaping, mission-directing revelation from God. It's a good thing they did or many of us might not be "in Christ." Let me explain.

The apostle Peter, a proud Jew, struggled with racism. His warped theological convictions led him to believe that Jews were superior to Gentiles. Then one day Peter received a revelatory vision from God that shattered his rationale for racism. While up on a roof, Peter fell into a trance. He had a vision of a sheet full of animals and birds that were considered sinful to eat according to Jewish Law. You can check out the interesting details of the story in Acts 10.

God used this odd vision to free Peter from his racist posture toward non-Jews. Then God led Peter to share the good news about Christ in the home of Cornelius, a Gentile! Peter confessed in the presence of these Gentiles, "I now realize how true it is that God does not show favoritism but accepts from every nation the one who fears him and does what is right" (Acts 10:34–35). Cornelius and everyone in his household came to faith in Christ. Gentiles, then and now, are part of the Christian movement because Peter was open to a theology-shattering revelation from God.

Where would we Gentiles be if those early Jewish Christians, indoctrinated from birth to view non-Jews as inferior, had missed or resisted this new revelation from God? The inclusion of Gentiles into the church might have never happened! Peter, in Mark's gospel, often missed revelation, but he eventually embraced a revelation that challenged his preferences and perspectives regarding Gentiles.

DEISM, DIVERSION, AND DISTRACTION

God's best days are not behind him. He is not some washed-up, forty-year-old professional baseball player. God still shows up to speak up in powerful ways. But, then again, does he really? Many of us often wonder if he truly does. We think to ourselves and maybe say to others, "God doesn't reveal anything to me." This might

God has allowed circumstances in my life to be prolonged until I listen to him. When I let go of certain things, I am free to listen to him and understand the whys.

—Nancy

reveal (pun intended) more about us than it does about God. Maybe we have become like the clueless disciples who missed revelation or the defiant religious leaders who resisted it. I wonder if we've been influenced by the perfect storm of 3D: deism, diversion, and distraction. Three-D is the culprit for the conversion of many would-be disciples into cultural churchianity.

DEISM

History is an insightful teacher. The church has gained so much from the modern period but lost something, too. We lost a healthy sort of mysticism that opens our eyes to the many ways God shows up to speak up among us. During the age of reason that surfaced in the seventeenth century, rationality was idolized while religion was minimized, even demonized. Many were convinced that truth could be discovered only through the human capacity for logical reasoning.

This cultural trend seeped into the church. The church became more analytical and logical and less intuitive and mystical. Many in the church became deists. They believed that God created and set the world in motion but was no longer personally engaged in the world. Deists believed God wound the cosmic clock and then took off. He wouldn't show up to speak up anymore. To deists God was like a father who leaves a million dollars in the bank to provide for his family and runs off never to be seen or heard from again.

I think the church is still recovering from the age of reason. Deism is more subtle today than it was four hundred years ago, but it is just as dangerous. The deism of churchianity is evident in the unstated, often unconscious, belief that everything God has already revealed is all he will ever reveal. God revealed himself through creation, Christ, and the biblical Canon, and then vanished. God closed the book on his interaction with humanity, so says the churchian deist. Many in the church today maintain deistic presuppositions without even realizing it.

Those who hold to deistic beliefs will miss or resist revelation from God. If we are going to walk by faith and not by sight, fresh revelation from God is crucial. The fresh revelation will always align with what God has already made known through creation, Christ, and the Canon, but it will offer a new angle of insight or application.

DIVERSION AND DISTRACTION

A contemporary form of deism is not the only barrier that blocks revelation. The majority of us battle the barriers of diversion and distraction. "If [a person] were happy, he would be the more so, the less he was diverted, like the Saints and God."[1] This observation was made by Blaise Pascal, a seventeenth-century French mathematician, scientist, philosopher, and theologian, long before diversions and distractions like Facebook, Twitter, and smartphones were conceived. Diversion and distraction are not novel temptations for the human race, but the intensity of their lure has certainly increased over the past few decades.

Too often churchians squeeze the self-revealing God out of the margins of life. We work longer hours. When we're not working, we're texting or tweeting. When we're not pushing characters on our phone or keyboard, we're taking in music or a movie. We go from one thing to the next, diverted and distracted. God is still on a quest to reveal himself to us, but spacious margins are often necessary to see and hear him.

God's revelation is like those works of art that look like simple dots but actually contain a hidden picture. You have to stop and stare at the image for a little while before you really see it. We will miss out on revelation from God if we don't develop the capacity to stop and stare.

CONTEMPORARY CENTURIONS

Why are those outside the church, people like the centurion and Cornelius, more open to revelation from God than some of us inside the church? Have we lost our sense of mystical wonder at the ways God reveals himself to us? Why are people outside the church often more prone than some inside the church to ask, "Is this a sign from God?" I realize that the unchurched don't have enough of a handle on God's revealed will in Scripture to check and validate their mystical impressions, but we must admit that their openness and wonder is admirable.

Maybe God is revealing a direction he wants you to go that will liberate some person or group, some neighborhood or nation. Maybe God is trying to reveal something that will free you from the jail cell that confines you. If you've not developed the capacity to receive revelation from God when he shows up to speak up, you just might miss out on something big, even something cosmic!

GOD TEARS IT UP

The good news is that, despite our slowness of revelatory reception, God keeps showing up among us. As Jean-Pierre de Caussade wrote, "Everything proclaims him to you, everything reveals him to you, everything brings him to you. He is by your side, over you, around and in you."[2] God will do whatever it takes to reveal himself to us. He will tear open the heavens (see Mark 1) and the sixty-foot-long, four-inch-thick temple curtain (see Mark 15). What barrier needs to be torn open for you to receive a fresh revelation from God?

We worship a God who became "flesh, and dwelt among us" (John 1:14 KJV). Jesus Christ is proof that God is "not far from any one of us" (Acts 17:27). God wants to interact with us, so much so that he became human in Christ to dwell among us. If you and I are going to experience true depth, we must be replenished and guided, inspired and illumined by identity-shaping and mission-directing revelation from God. But how?

As I was listening to a pastor talk about parenting, God revealed something to me. He showed me that the focus of my discipleship of others at home and work was based more on information about God than an experience of him. It became immediately clear that my efforts and prayers should be directed toward positioning those I lead to experience God's power, rather than simply giving them more head knowledge about God. As this revelation has taken root, God has used it to transform my life as well as the lives of those I lead.

—Jeff

FORMATION THROUGH REVELATION

We simply must apply advice we have heard since childhood. Although the guidance was clear, it was hard for a hyperactive, easily distracted kid like me to apply. The complexities of adulthood make this childlike wisdom even more challenging to live out. Here is the mandate: Stop, look, and listen.

Simple, right? The people who encounter God's self-revealing presence and power are Christians with the capacity to stop, look, and listen. The best Christians are not the best talkers; they are the best listeners. They know how to stop, look, and listen for the God who dwells among us.

PRACTICAL MATTERS

Revelatory reception does not come naturally or happen accidentally. The people who see and hear God when he shows up to speak up adopt practices that help them to stop, look, and listen. They might reflect daily and deeply by journaling their prayers to God in light of their circumstances. Through the words of their own pen, God reveals himself. They might consistently take a day alone with God every month not just to voice their prayer to God, but to listen for God's revelation to them. They might designate two to three annual vacation days for a retreat of silence and solitude, perhaps even at a monastery. They might read books written not by twenty-first-century methodological masters but by seventeenth-century French mystics like Brother Lawrence, whose wisdom is presented in *The Practice of the Presence of God*, and Jean-Pierre de Caussade, author of *The Sacrament of the Present Moment*. Certainly they intentionally seek out a spiritual director and a band of brothers or sisters who can help them to stop, look, and listen for God in the contours of life's journey. And they refuse to distance themselves from the local church, even when they want to, but instead lean into life together in Christian community. These people engage in any and every Christian spiritual discipline that will increase their capacity to stop, look, and listen for the revelation of God among us.

Stopping, looking, and listening are lost arts for twenty-first-century Christians who are constantly on the go. So, we settle for shortcuts. We hunt for cutting-edge trends that promise discipleship gain without pain. We have relied, I think, on others who stop, look, and listen to tell us what they saw and heard from God. This only perpetuates the spread of shallow churchianity.

How do we facilitate the practice of stopping, looking, and listening? First, we need to stop. Clear the clutter. Since we're already onto seventeenth-century French Christians, let's hear again from Pascal. He wrote, "I have discovered that all the unhappiness of men arises from one single fact, that they cannot stay quietly in their own chamber."[3] Pascal was right. Diversion prohibits reflection on matters of ultimate significance. Stop the obsession with diversions and distractions, such as Facebook, Twitter, Instagram, e-mail, and texting. Stop regretting the past. Stop stressing about the future. Stop and experience the fullness of the present moment through which God comes to us. *Stop!*

Once we stop, we can begin to look at God's revelation among us. When you stop to look, you see not just an early morning sunrise, but also a revelatory reminder that God's Son will rise in the mourning of your loss. When you look, you see not just a newborn baby, but also a revelation of the God who makes all things new. When you look, you see not just an entertaining movie called *Forest Gump*, but also a revelation from the God who liberates you to liberate others. When you stop to look, you see God dwelling among you in all kinds of ways. *Look!*

As we stop to look, our other senses come alive. We become "all ears" and can really listen. When we listen to the words behind the words of people, we often get a revelation from God. When you hear one of your children say out of the blue, "Even when it rains I still love God," you hear a revelatory challenge to love God even, and especially when, life rains down pain. When you hear a grunge band yell their way through a four-minute song, you don't just hear rebellious angst, you hear a revelation from God to live your life in a way that presents a peace-filled alternative. When a colleague critiques you harshly, you don't hear jealous insecurity, you hear God say almost audibly, "Be humble and stay teachable." When the minister offers a long-winded pastoral prayer during the service, your mind doesn't drift to what you will eat for lunch, it focuses on the God who reveals the person you should invite to lunch. *Listen!*

How do we know if the revelation originated from God or from the thin air of our own thoughts? Here are a few helpful guidelines: If the revelation aligns with and does not contradict Scripture, it's probably from God. If you have nothing to gain from the revelation but the glory of God and the well-being of someone else, it's probably from God. If the revelation has the potential to cultivate holiness in you or others, it's probably from God. These guidelines are the guardrails within which divine revelation tends to travel. God still provides revelation that humanity desperately needs to see Jesus more clearly and understand our mission more fully. Mark's gospel presents a God who will stop at nothing to reveal what matters most. The author of Hebrews wrote that God "is the same yesterday and today and forever" (Heb. 13:8), which means he still wants to be found. He may reveal himself through a verse, person, image, prayer, book, retreat, trial, or some other way.

Sadly, we will resist that revelation if deism gets the best of us. And we will miss it if we are constantly diverted and distracted. If we stop, look, and listen, however, we can develop the spiritual ability to discern and embrace life-giving revelations from God.

I was in my backyard one morning, praying over some decisions I had to make. I sensed no direction. Then I looked up and saw one half of a rainbow arch. I asked God, "If your answer to the question about my decision is 'yes,' let me see the rest of the rainbow appear." *Bam!* Immediately the rest of the rainbow appeared. I noticed that all of the colors weren't visible. I asked God to show me the colors. As soon as I did, all of the colors appeared. I stood in awe of God. He showed up in my backyard to show himself strong on my behalf.

—Debby

IMPLICATIONS OF REVELATION

I am no hero of revelatory reception. I have missed or resisted more divine revelations than I care to admit, and more than I likely even realize. Perhaps one of God's most gracious graces is the one that keeps us from recognizing how many revelations from him have gone right over our heads.

But there have been a few instances when I leaned in to the grace to stop, look, and listen for God's revelation. I have felt most alive when God ripped through the temple curtain that was blinding me in order to reveal himself. These revelations changed the course of my life, led me to fruitful mission, and induced a confident hope in God. One such revelation was in the fall semester of my senior year of college when I started to date Abby. She wasn't my first flame during those collegiate years, but I was kind of hoping she might be my last. I was ready to settle down. Abby seemed perfect in many ways, but she wasn't perfect for me. I knew this but ignored it. Then one day, I knelt down in my small bedroom on campus to pray. I finally stopped, looked, and listened. God showed up to speak up. I sensed God saying as clearly as though with words to my ears, "Break up with Abby and grow in contentment with me."

The revelation was crystal clear. I couldn't disregard it, despite my fear of breaking up with Abby. So I did what any guy in my shoes would do: I blamed God. "God told me that we should break up," I said to Abby, almost apologizing for God. She laughed and walked away, seemingly relieved by my words. Too relieved, really. Perhaps God had given the same revelation to her.

Here's where the revelation really paid off. I grew in contentment with God. I fell in love with him and, therefore, didn't need to look for love in all the wrong places. While I was looking for God, I met a woman named Amy. She became my friend. Then, in a few years, she became my wife. Amy is not only as close to perfect as anyone I know, she is perfect for me. And I might have missed her if I had not stopped, looked, and listened long enough for God to show up and speak up.

Sometime later I received another truly astounding revelation from God. This time I was a full-time graduate student at a seminary in Kentucky. I was also pastoring part time at a local church. The "D-mons" of diversion and distraction were having their way with me. My prayer life was horribly inconsistent, but I managed to pray once in a while. One midweek day, late morning, I found myself kneeling to stop, look, and listen. And, as you may have guessed, God showed up to speak up.

I don't recall what I was praying about, but my older sister Tammy popped into my mind. She was not a Christian. She is a tough-as-nails woman, born and bred on the mean streets of South Philadelphia. Men had frequently disappointed her. She got divorced in her twenties. Tammy was starving for love.

I had been telling Tammy about Christ's love for over a decade, ever since my conversion. At one point she asked me, with obvious agitation in her voice, to "stop stuffing God" down her throat. I respected her request until the day of revelation.

As I prayed for Tammy, God spoke to a place deep within my soul and said, "Tell her that I am the Mr. Right she is looking for. I will never dump or divorce her. She is the apple of my eye."

I argued with God. "God, I've already told her many times that you love her. She doesn't want to hear it any longer. I don't want to push her further away." God persisted. I submitted.

I wrote Tammy a letter, telling her that Jesus was the Mr. Right who would never leave or forsake her. I mailed the letter and, to be honest, forgot all about it. I really didn't expect much good to come of it. Faith does not come easily for me.

Three days later, I received a call from Tammy. My stoic sister was crying. She informed me that her boyfriend, the one she had hoped to marry, had just left her. This break-up happened between my sending the letter and her receiving it. She was disappointed once again by a man she thought was her Mr. Right. After telling me about her pain, Tammy spoke words I never thought I would hear from her mouth. She said, "Len, I need Mr. Right. I need Jesus." What? Did a space invader take over my sister?

During a small window of time, my sister was open to the idea of entering into a relationship with Christ. God knew when the window to my sister's heart would be open, even if only a crack. He sent me a revelation to give to her a life-giving, hope-inducing word from him. If I had not accessed the grace to stop, look, and listen, I would have totally missed this opportunity that brought my sister a significant step closer to Christ, the ultimate Mr. Right.

> One night while I was reading the Bible, God revealed that he was calling me to the counseling profession. Then he confirmed my calling the following week through a music festival.
>
> —Crystal

Revelation matters. Here is one more powerful example that shows why. One of our children had some major health issues surface when he was four. I won't go into all of the details, but Amy and I were stunned. We researched his symptoms, talked to doctor after doctor, and prayed for him fervently. After about eighteen months, I cracked. I became withdrawn and depressed. I was frustrated by my inability to do anything to help my struggling son. I stopped praying. Prayer reminded me of my son's struggle. I wanted an escape from my reality.

Then one day I stopped, looked, and listened. I was teaching an elective course for Wesley Seminary called "Spiritual Retreat for the Leader." Twenty-two students joined me onsite at the Abbey of

Gethsemane in Kentucky. During one of the days at the abbey, I mandated a fast from talking. We devoted the entire day to silence and solitude, so that we could stop, look, and listen for God.

I went for a walk in the woods, trying my best not to think of my suffering son or anything else that might induce stress, such as the number of student papers waiting for me to grade. All of a sudden, out of nowhere, an image entered my mind. I saw Christ riding a white horse out on the plains of the western frontier. He noticed a beautiful piece of land and threw his long wooden stake into that piece of property. Christ staked his claim. Just when I was about to check my forehead for a fever and dismiss this odd image, I sensed God saying to me, "Your son is mine. He's my territory. I stake my claim on his life. I've got him."

Now, I could have concluded that the monastic cheese I had eaten was rotten to excuse this vision. That was, in fact, my first guess. My second one was that the monk-made fudge, which tasted more like bourbon than fudge, was the culprit for that strange vision. I could easily dismiss the image that way. Or, I could receive it as a revelatory gift from God. And after pondering it all, that's what I did. Now when I start to worry about my son, that image of the stake-claiming Christ calms my fears. The God who claimed my child as his own will not let anyone or anything take that territory.

Is this the wishful thinking of a desperate dad or a revelation from God? All I know is that this odd image replaced my pain with God's peace. God used it to give me perspective I didn't have before that revelatory image surfaced. What I said with my mouth, I now knew deep in my soul: My children belong to God. God's love for my children exceeds my love for them. He has staked his claim on their lives. This revelation has saved me from the unbearable worry and depression that was suffocating me.

We can get better rather than bitter as we grow older. The bitter path leans into a cultural churchianity that perpetuates deism, diversion, and distraction. The better path leads to a biblical Christianity that cultivates the capacity to stop, look, and listen for the God who shows up to speak up. God's revelations shape our true identity over time. He says, "This is my son or daughter, whom I love." God's revelations also lead us to places of missional impact. Through an odd rooftop vision, God sent Jewish Peter on a mission to Gentile Cornelius. That revelation changed everything, then and now.

Manna doesn't store well. It is not always enough to rely on yesterday's manna of revelation. If we are going to swim in the deep end of discipleship, we need to stop, look, and listen for fresh manna, life-giving bread from heaven, as God reveals himself.

SWIMMING PRINCIPLE

When we stop, look, and listen for the God who shows up to speak up, we will receive identity-shaping and mission-directing revelation.

SWIMMING PRACTICE

When was the last time God revealed something to you?

How do you or can you stop, look, and listen for God to show up to speak up?

Over the next week, practice journaling. Pick a time of day when you are most alert to write in your journal. Reflect with your pen on how God has been showing up to speak up to you.

Take a monthly day alone with God over the next three months. The goal is to carve out six to eight hours to intensely stop, look, and listen for God to show up and speak up. Bring your Bible, journal, a few soul-enriching books, and some soothing music.

SWIMMER'S PRAYER

Lord, we need a revelation from you that reminds us of who we are, whose we are, and what we are called to do. Forgive us for the deism, distraction, and diversion that block our eyes from seeing you and our ears from hearing you. Increase our capacity to stop, look, and listen for you to show up and speak up. It is impossible for us to become the people you call us to be and do the work you have called us to do without revelation from you that shapes our identity and guides our mission. Lord, reveal yourself to us. Amen.

NOTES

1. Blaise Pascal, "170," *Pensées*, accessed November 29, 2014, http://www.gutenberg.org/files/18269/18269-h/18269-h.htm.

2. Jean-Pierre de Caussade, *The Sacrament of the Present Moment*, trans. Kitty Muggeridge (San Francisco: HarperCollins, 1989), 18.

3. Pascal, *Pensées*, "139."

RESTORATION
WHAT GOD DOES FOR US

3

I'm an atrocious golfer. One time three women in their seventies watched me tee off. I swung my driver as hard as I could and the ball went about two feet. Those kind women invited me to hit another shot. I did. This time I crushed the ball, hitting it about 250 yards. The ball went straight for fifty yards and then sliced two hundred yards to the right. I stepped aside, disgraced, and let the women play through. All three hit their first shots perfectly off the tee, straight as an arrow and with good distance. They were grinning with delight. I was humiliated!

There was also one time I swung my 6-iron from the fairway and the ball actually traveled backward a few inches. Many times I have swung the club as hard as I could, missing the ball completely, before lifting my head to see if anyone noticed. Someone usually did. If thick woods loom anywhere nearby, my ball will find them. If water stands between me and the green, my ball will find it.

I need mulligans—do-overs—most of the time. A mulligan allows a golfer to play from the spot of a previous bad stroke without penalty. You act as if the errant shot never happened. A mulligan is a second chance.

After twenty-two years of golfing, I still need mulligans in my game. After forty-two years of living, I keep needing mulligans in my life! Who doesn't?

47

PETER NEEDED A MULLIGAN

The apostle Peter needed a mulligan. Peter played most of his discipleship game not on the beautiful fairway leading to the hole, but in the rough surrounded by obstacles. He lofted his share of really good shots from the tee, but those were usually followed by horrendous approach shots. This is the pattern plastered all over Mark's gospel. Let's look at a few examples of Peter's pattern.

The first half of the gospel of Mark focuses on Jesus' identity. Mark clued in the reader on who Jesus is in 1:1. Jesus is the "Messiah, the Son of God." In Mark 8:27–33, we find Jesus conversing with the apostles about his identity. After he asked, "Who do people say I am?" (v. 27), Jesus probed with the more pointed question, "Who do you say I am?" (v. 29). No one was ready to offer an answer except for Peter. He replied, "You are the Messiah" (v. 29)! Peter was right on. He crushed the ball, hitting it three hundred yards right down the middle of the fairway!

Peter was beginning to understand Jesus' identity. He whiffed, though, on Jesus' mission. Jesus revealed that he was on a death mission to Jerusalem. Peter didn't like the sound of that. He had a better one in mind for Jesus. He was probably hoping for a mission that would lead to political power and prosperity. His desire was "par for the course" among Jews of that day.

Thus, after Jesus described his mission of suffering, Peter rebuked him. What was Peter thinking? Jesus responded bluntly, "Get behind me, Satan! . . . You do not have in mind the concerns of God, but merely human concerns" (v. 33). Peter hit the ball into the rough, and there were five trees obstructing a direct shot to the green.

This was Peter's pattern. He hit a fantastic shot with the correct answer, then botched the next one. But Peter could still play out of the mess he had created.

In Mark 10:17–31, Peter's pattern surfaces again. Jesus invited a wealthy man into an adventurous discipleship journey. In order to join Jesus, the man had to shed his attachment to money. He refused, but, when faced with the same requirement, Peter had not. "We have left everything to follow you" (v. 28) Peter reminded Jesus. The sacrifices Peter made to follow Jesus were substantial. Peter left the fishing business and his family. He left the familiar. He left all to follow Jesus, the radical rabbi. Peter compared himself to the rich man and looked good.

But Jesus rained on Peter's parade. While Peter was patting himself on the back, Jesus essentially said to Peter, "You can't outgive God." What Peter had sacrificed for Christ was nothing compared to what Christ would sacrifice for him. Peter hit the discipleship ball into the rough again, but, again, he could still play out of the mess.

Peter's pattern emerges yet another time in Mark 14. Peter first hit a fantastic shot, according to 14:27–31. Jesus predicted that the Twelve, upon his impending arrest, would all fall away. Peter could not let Jesus' prediction pass. He boasted, "Even if all fall away, I will not" (v. 29). Then Jesus foretold Peter's three-time denial. The apostle became even more emphatic: "Even if I have to die with you, I will never disown you" (v. 31). What commitment! What courage! What confidence! Once more Peter spoke up and shone brightly. He said what the rest of the apostles wished they had the guts to say. He crushed that ball off the tee, straight down the fairway about three hundred yards and onto the green. The best part was that his eleven buddies saw him do it.

You know by now what's coming. Peter promised that he would die rather than disown Jesus, a promise that put Peter on the green a foot from the hole. But he ruined that hole with a humiliating three-putt! Peter said he would die for Jesus, but he couldn't even stay awake for him (see Mark 14:32–42).

Jesus had urged Peter, James, and John to "keep watch" (v. 34). However, Peter and the other two fell asleep not once or twice, but three times. There's the three-putt. Three times Peter let Jesus down, just as Jesus was preparing to give his life for Peter and the world. Jesus, after tirelessly investing in Peter for three years, asked his friend to keep watch, and Peter couldn't even stay awake. Peter failed his friend Jesus when Jesus needed a friend most.

It's easy to recover from the failure of falling asleep. Sometimes we're just too tired to stay awake. No big deal. Peter was, however, about to hit a shot from which it would be nearly impossible to recover. He three-putted again, but not by falling asleep. This time Peter denied three times that he even knew Jesus. This sad stroke is recorded in Mark 14:66–72. Peter sliced the ball of his life deep into the woods. There was no way he could play out of this debacle.

Golf is frustrating. It's not for the faint of heart. I heard about a guy who was having a terrible day at the course. He hit one dreadful shot after another. Finally, toward the end of the round, he had enough. He walked over to one of the ponds, lifted his golf bag over his head, and threw it as far as he could into the water. He walked away, mumbling to himself and jerking his head erratically. Then he stopped. He turned back and walked toward the pond. He went into the pond and found his bag. He lifted the bag and unzipped one of its pockets. He recovered his car keys, threw the bag back in the pond, and drove home. I suspect he gave up on the game of golf forever.

Peter threw his bag of clubs into the pond as well. He was tired of his inconsistent discipleship swing and ready to throw in the towel. There are indications, especially in John's gospel, that Peter was about to quit the risky business of fishing for people and return to the safe predictability of fishing for fish (see John 21). Sorrow and pain due to his denial of Jesus overwhelmed Peter. "He broke down and wept" (Mark 14:72) because of his miserable failure, his irrevocable shot. He had sliced his discipleship ball deep into the woods. I wonder if Peter said to himself what I might have said to myself: "I will never be able to become the rock Jesus thinks I am. I will never overcome my proclivity toward prideful arrogance. I will never have a walk with Christ that exceeds my talk. I am done with the mission and will return to fishin'. I will return to churchianity, which is neither meaningful nor adventurous, but is safe within the bounds of what I can handle."

> I had come to the end of myself. I hated everyone, mostly myself.
>
> —Alice

Peter needed a mulligan, a do-over, a clean slate, a fresh start.

WE NEED MULLIGANS TOO

Tiger Woods is one of the most talented golfers in the history of the sport. He, no doubt, thought he would never again need a mulligan. But he did. He sliced the ball of his life so deep into the woods that many people wondered if he would ever find it.

Woods scored below seventy in a round of golf when he was only twelve years old. For those of you who don't know golf, that's outstanding. When he was twenty-one, he became the youngest player ever to win the Masters Tournament. He was the first person to be named *Sports Illustrated*'s Athlete of the Year more than once. He was also the first athlete to earn more than one billion dollars.

Life, for him, was like living on a fantastic fairway and gorgeous green. Then he sliced the ball of his life into the woods. On November 25, 2009, a tabloid claimed that Woods, a married man with two children, had an affair. Two days later, Woods ran his car into a tree while trying to escape from his angry wife, who was attacking him with a golf club. On December 2, *US Weekly* released a voicemail message from Woods's alleged mistress. He immediately went public, admitting his transgressions and asking the media to respect his family's privacy. Over the next few days, more than a dozen women came forward claiming they also had affairs with Woods. On December 11, he issued another statement, apologizing for his infidelity and announcing he was taking a hiatus from golf.

Woods lost millions of dollars in endorsements. He is no longer golf's clean-cut poster player. People don't look at him the same way. There is no going back. Woods sliced the ball of his life deep into the woods. I wonder if he is still looking for the ball and trying to play out, or if he has given up completely.

While our slices likely haven't cost us millions or been so public, we can relate to Tiger and Peter. We need mulligans too. Our need for a mulligan comes in two ways. We tend to (1) replay the regrettable slices of the past and (2) recommit the sinful slices of the present. Both types of slices are destructive for disciples.

When we replay the regrettable failures of the past, we live in guilt and stay stuck in the woods. Most of us have hit at least one tragic "shot" in our past, one that we are tempted to replay over and over again. This past regret might be a bad decision you made that caused you or someone else immense pain. You said something that severely damaged or totally destroyed a relationship. You had an affair. You quit a good job. You stole some cash. You took a sip. You got high. You dropped out of school. You gossiped about a friend. You bought a house you couldn't afford. You said no to a mission from God. You got divorced.

In the depths of our souls, we replay our past regrettable slices, when the ball of our lives ended up in the woods. Most of us have discovered that past regrets can prevent present progress. It's paralyzing.

We not only replay the regrettable slices of the past, we tend to recommit the sinful slices in the present. You look at porn again. You fly off the handle again. You speak damaging words again. You make the wrong choice again. You betray a friend again. You get drunk again. You skip your devotional time again. You are overcome by pride again. You withhold your time and treasure from someone who needs both again. You make your special someone an idol again. You spend money you don't have again.

Your friends are intentionally finding ways to improve their discipleship golf. They recruit a golf coach, a mentor who can help them grow spiritually. They read golf-improvement books that help them correct their discipleship swing. Then they practice, practice, practice spiritual disciplines. Some of those friends have knocked dozens of strokes off their discipleship game. They need fewer and fewer mulligans.

Not you. You keep struggling with the same sinful slice. After five, ten, twenty, or more years, you still possess that same slice. You still struggle with the lust that plagued your game as a teenager. You still struggle with the arrogance that masks your insecurity. You still slice the shot of your life into the woods of anger, jealousy, greed, relational dysfunction, devotional inconsistency, sinful cynicism, materialism, or some other tangled area. It's the same old shot in the woods over and over and over again. Enough!

Replaying and recommitting our dismal shots can make us feel so low. Have you ever been so frustrated in your discipleship journey that you wanted to throw your golf clubs into the pond? Have you ever found yourself stuck in the woods, ready to settle for a mini-golf version of discipleship?

Perhaps you have internally, even subconsciously, concluded that you have taken way too many mulligans already. Your discipleship golf game has not improved over the years, but has plateaued or worsened. You are tired of not living up to discipleship standards. Internally, you wonder if you should just give up the hope of ever having a viable discipleship game.

> I grew up in a church that emphasized nonessentials. My desire was to serve God, but I viewed him as a God of justice. His mercy and grace were not factors in my understanding of his nature. I grew up serving God but not enjoying a loving relationship with him. Eventually, I was introduced to a God of love and mercy at a banquet. I listened to others testify about how God's love changed their lives. I was blown away.
>
> —Elaine

Are you ready to throw in your clubs? You might not stop following Jesus entirely, but maybe you find yourself following him from a distance. Are you tempted to settle for mini-golf, the discipleship of cultural churchianity. It's safe, predictable, and less disappointing. But it's also boring, meaningless, and incapable of fostering a fruitful and fulfilling discipleship journey. Are you ready to settle for life in the woods instead of on the fairway? Are you willing to give up the dream of becoming a real, radical, reliable, and rocklike disciple? If you find yourself in the woods, you know what it's like to be like Peter. You need a mulligan.

GOD GIVES MULLIGANS

Let's face it, some shots land in places we just can't play out of no matter how hard we try. We hope for a mulligan but can't give ourselves one. It must come as a gift of pure grace from someone else. Peter needed a gracious mulligan. He got one!

Perhaps the most important verse in the Bible for duffers like me is Mark 16:7. The power of this verse is subtle. Three women visited Jesus' tomb, but he was not there because he had risen from the dead. An angel told the women this good news. Of course angels say only what God sends them to say. Their message is directly from God, as if God himself were conveying the message.

Here's what the angel said to the women in Mark 16:7: "Go, tell his disciples and Peter, 'He is going ahead of you into Galilee. There you will see him, just as he told you.'" Did you catch it? God is sending Peter a mulligan through an angel's message to some women. Peter was probably not feeling much like a disciple. So the angel singled him out with the words "and Peter." Mulligan!

Peter's story reveals more about God than about Peter. God wanted to give Peter the mulligan Peter could never give himself. If you think I'm reading too much into Mark 16:7, let's remember that Mark got his gospel material from Peter. Mark was Peter's spiritual son. They met in Rome, where Mark recorded the gospel details he received from Peter. I imagine Peter remembering this story with tears in his eyes. "'And Peter.' That's what they told me the angel said, 'and Peter.' Mark, my son, it's as if the Lord went out of his way to let me know through an angel, 'I still want you, Peter. Here's a mulligan!'"

John's gospel describes the mulligan in a more direct and personal way (see 21:15–17). Jesus rose from the dead and eventually met up with Peter on the beach. Jesus gave Peter three chances to affirm his love. Three times Jesus asked Peter, "Do you love me?" Three times Peter affirmed his love for Jesus. Do you see what Jesus did? Peter had denied his love for Jesus three times before the crucifixion. That's a regrettable slice into the woods if ever there was one. But later Jesus gave Peter the chance to affirm his love for Jesus three times. Think about the math. A negative three (denials) plus a positive three (affirmations) equals zero. A fresh start. A clean slate. A do-over. A mulligan.

That's what a grace-filled mulligan looks like. It's so refreshing in a world where you get what you deserve, where what goes around comes around. In a grudge-holding, eye-for-eye and tooth-for-tooth type of world, a mulligan is so stunningly beautiful.

The mulligan concept is plastered all over the profound pages of the biblical story. In fact, the mulligan was built into the fabric of God's chosen Hebrew people. Here's how.

Some of the people sliced the ball of their lives into the woods financially. When they could not pay their debt with goods or livestock, they had to pay it with their land or freedom. They became landless or slaves or both.

God, in his wisdom, wanted to ensure that the socioeconomic system of his people prevented the poor from becoming so poor that they could lose everything. God wanted to prevent poverty from being perpetual. During the Year of Jubilee, which was supposed to occur every fifty years, slaves would be set free and land would be restored back to the family that gave it up to pay a debt. Mulligan!

The blowing of the ram's horn on the Day of Atonement, also called Yom Kippur, announced the jubilee. Yom Kippur was celebrated annually by the Jewish people and powerfully highlights the mulligan concept. Leviticus 16 describes the event in vivid detail. On the Day of Atonement, the high priest laid his hands on the head of a goat, called the scapegoat. The priest confessed his sins and then the sins of the entire nation. All of the sins of all the people committed all that year were transferred onto the scapegoat. The animal was led out of the city and into the desert, thus taking away the sins of the people. Every year on the Day of Atonement, the people got a do-over, a mulligan.

> I was trying to crawl out of a pit I had dug for myself. I couldn't. When I let go of the walls of that pit, God pulled me out of it. I finally understood grace. Once I got in touch with God's grace, I was able to live out of it instead of out of my own drives and motivations. Living out of grace molded my character for the better. Grace helped me get a handle on formerly abstract biblical concepts.
>
> —J.B.

Jesus is our ultimate jubilee. He is our Yom Kippur. He is our scapegoat. He is our mulligan. Christians are mulligan-shaped people. Yet tragically so many of us are still trying to pull ourselves up by the bootstraps and play out of the woods on our own. We can't. Some have given up on the hope of ever being on the fairway again.

Take the mulligan! Don't refuse it. If you cannot receive a restorative mulligan from God when you slice the ball of your life into the woods, you will stay stuck in the woods forever. Too many

Christians remain stuck in the woods due to the guilt of past regrets and present failures. They refuse to grab the grace-infused mulligan.

We may have to endure some of the consequences of past and present slices into the woods, but make no mistake—God gives mulligans. "Because of the LORD's great love we are not consumed, for his compassions never fail" (Lam. 3:22). "As far as the east is from the west, so far has he removed our transgressions from us" (Ps. 103:12). "If we confess our sins, he is faithful and just and will forgive us our sins and purify us from all unrighteousness" (1 John 1:9). "Tell his disciples *and Peter*" (Mark 16:7, emphasis added). Sounds like God still gives mulligans!

MULLIGANS RESTORE US

What became of Peter after the mulligan? Mark's gospel never tells us, but Luke does in the book of Acts. The same Peter, who cowardly denied knowing Jesus three times boldly proclaimed Jesus' lordship. Peter said to thousands of Jews, "This Jesus, whom you crucified, [is] both Lord and Messiah" (Acts 2:36). How do you explain this transformation? What happened between the cowardice and the courage? A mulligan!

Peter, like most Jews of his day, struggled with racism. He believed that Jews were superior to Gentiles. But Acts 10:34–35 tells us Peter stood in the home of a Gentile and professed, "I now realize how true it is that God does not show favoritism but accepts from every nation the one who fears him and does what is right." How do you explain Peter's shift from racist exclusion to radical inclusion? A mulligan!

A mulligan is not some cheap form of grace, an excuse to keep on sinning. The person who fully embraces the mulligan of grace will be radically restored by it. The mulligan takes the disciple out of the woods and places him or her on the fairway. Mulligans aren't excuses or enablers. They are not simply a second chance. They are game changers. Mulligans change people.

The mulligan knocked many strokes off Peter's game. He overcame the patterns that plagued him. He eventually lived up to his name, which means "stone or rock." The thing that transformed Peter was not his skill, intellect, or ingenuity. A mulligan of grace from God turned Simon into Peter.

We all slice the ball of our lives into the woods from time to time. When we do, Jesus hands us another ball and says, "Take a mulligan." The mulligan will make us better. It will knock a dozen strokes off our discipleship game. Disciples of true depth realize their dependence upon grace-filled mulligans, without which they would stay stuck. And, over time, they would become comfortable where they are.

I was replaying a regrettable slice of my past that caused me to recommit a sinful slice in the present. Here I was, a seminary student with a few years of pastoral ministry under my belt, and I desperately needed a mulligan. I was stuck in the woods, bound by my own guilt. I was tempted to give up on the hope of becoming a radical and rocklike disciple. I needed help. I needed a golf coach.

Dr. Reg Johnson was my spiritual formation professor at Asbury Theological Seminary. I respected him immensely. He embodied the kind of prayerful, wise, humble, and disciplined disciple I hoped to become. I recruited him to be my discipleship golf coach, but I hesitated to share how I had sliced the ball of my life into the woods. I didn't want him to think less of me when I thought so much of him.

> God has brought me to my knees many times over. I keep walking away or turning my back on him. But he keeps reminding me that he is not finished with me. As long as I am open and looking to him for what I need, he will guide my every step.
>
> —Deb

During one of our monthly mentoring meetings, I came clean and confessed to Reg some of my past regrets that were fostering present failures. There was no way I could play out of this mess. I was not convinced that someone like me, already forgiven, could be forgiven again. I was trapped.

Reg, sensing my desperation, did something I will never forget. He slid his chair closer to mine, put his hands on my shoulders, looked me square in the eyes, and said slowly, "Lenny, in the name of Jesus Christ, you are forgiven."

Those words, and the manner in which he expressed them, were a musical mulligan to my ears. I needed that to get out of the discipleship woods. Finally, I was back on the victorious fairway.

What can you do to play out of the woods? Are there five simple steps for getting back on the fairway? Nope! The application of this chapter has little to do with you and a lot to do with God. Here is the primary application for you—take a mulligan. If you have sliced the ball of your life so deep into the woods you can't find it or play out of the mess, get past your self-mutilating pride. Accept a mulligan. In the name of Jesus Christ, you are forgiven!

SWIMMING PRINCIPLE

God provides restorative grace-filled mulligans for us when we slice the ball of our lives into the woods.

SWIMMING PRACTICE

What regrettable slices of your past are you tempted to replay?

What sinful slices in the present are you most prone to recommit?

Describe a gracious mulligan you have received from someone. What impact did it have on you?

Mulligan getters are mulligan givers. Describe a time when you extended a grace-filled mulligan to someone. What impact did it have on you and on that person?

Do you know of someone who is currently stuck in the woods? How might God want to use you to extend a mulligan to that person?

SWIMMER'S PRAYER

Lord of the mulligan, too many of us have given up the hope of ever having a viable discipleship golf game. Too many of us have settled for mini-golf. We are tempted to replay the regrettable shots of the past or recommit the sinful shots in the present. Either one adversely impacts our walk with you. Today we will embrace the grace-filled mulligan you offer so that we are restored to the deep intimacy and discipleship vitality we crave in you. Amen.

TRANSFORMATION 4

WHAT GOD DOES TO US

I don't like meat loaf. I find it bland. Soon after Amy and I were married, she started to develop her arsenal of recipes. Her goal was to broaden my dietary horizons. My goal was to enjoy familiar foods, like the meals my mom prepared. The honeymoon was over as soon as it was, well, over.

To my dismay, Amy discovered a recipe for meat loaf. What's worse, she was going to try it out on me. I did what only a naïve newlywed male would dare to do. I voiced my displeasure. Amy was gracious. She said, "Just give it a try; I'm sure you'll like it." She was confident. I was doubtful.

Amy brought that ordinary ground beef, cryptically disguised as a loaf of meat to the table. It was not what I expected. It didn't look like plain old ground beef. Peppers and onions peeked out of (and were probably wanting out of) the lump of shredded cattle. A combination of cheeses oozed from the beefy mound. I was not ready to admit defeat at that point in my marriage, but my nose and eyes were surprisingly delighted.

My skepticism concerning my wife's predicted "I'm sure you'll like it" diminished. I boldly took a bite. It tasted as good as it smelled and better than it looked. It was delicious. Best meat loaf ever. In my wife's miracle-working hands, ordinary ground beef became an extraordinary meat loaf!

GOD MAKES THE ORDINARY EXTRAORDINARY

What my wife does with ground beef, Jesus did with something more ordinary and less spectacular. He did it with bread, unleavened bread at that! "While they were eating, Jesus took bread, and when he had given thanks, he broke it and gave it to his disciples, saying, 'Take it; this is my body'" (Mark 14:22).

Frederick Buechner wrote, "You enter the extraordinary by way of the ordinary."[1] Perhaps this is why ordinary elements like bread and wine are the raw ingredients for something much more extraordinary. Maybe this is why a seemingly ordinary peasant Jew born to peasant parents living in a peasant town would lead humanity into the extraordinary kingdom of God.

Jesus transformed ordinary bread into his extraordinary body through three distinct actions—by taking it, breaking it, and giving it.

Mark tells us that this happened during the Passover Feast (see Mark 14:12). The Passover commemorates the exodus event, which took place about fourteen hundred years before Jesus' Last Supper with the Twelve. Back then, the poor and uneducated Hebrew people were slaves to the elite Egyptians. Then God showed up. He *passed over* the land, punishing the Egyptian oppressors and protecting the Hebrew slaves. God took into his hands ordinary, lackluster slaves.

God eventually transformed these ordinary slaves into something extraordinary. They became a holy nation, a royal priesthood, the Israelites. He took ordinary slaves out of Egypt and gave them to Canaan as an extraordinary nation. Between the taking of slaves from the land of bondage and leading them into the Promised Land, something extraordinary happened: transformation.

More than a thousand years later, in Mark 14, God is up to something big again. As Jesus celebrated the Passover Feast with the apostles, he was forming a group of ordinary people into something more extraordinary than they were at the time. He transformed this group through a new act of grace, a new covenant.

What happened to the bread in the hands of Christ at that meal ultimately happened to those who shared the meal with him. That night Christ not only took ordinary bread and gave it new meaning as representing his extraordinary body, but he took ordinary odorous fishermen, violently opinionated zealots, and a greedy tax collector in order to give them to the world as extraordinary apostolic leaders of the church.

Like my wife with ground beef, Jesus works miracles. In his hands, the ordinary become extraordinary, lepers become cleansed, the lame become walkers, prostitutes become chaste, tax collectors become generous, and sinners become saints. Even Simon became Peter, and Saul became Paul.

Today, the hands of Christ still work miracles. He transforms the ordinary into the extraordinary. He takes a high-school dropout alcoholic and gives him to the world as a pastor. He takes a greedy CEO and gives her as a generous philanthropist. He takes a demoralized divorcee and gives her as a missionary to China. He takes a political criminal and gives him as a minister to the incarcerated. He takes a mafia member and gives him as an evangelist. He takes a sheltered churchgoer and gives her as a friend to urban prostitutes. Real people. Real transformation. Christ takes ordinary bread and gives it to the church as his extraordinary body.

BUT HOW DOES GOD TRANSFORM?

The ordinary is transformed into the extraordinary. But how? What happened between the taking of the bread and the giving of Jesus' body? What happened between the taking of some Hebrew slaves from Egypt and the giving of the Israelite nation to Canaan? What happened between the taking of common men and the giving of apostolic leaders who would change the world?

Between the taking and the giving is the breaking. Jesus took the bread, broke the bread, and then gave the bread as the representation of his body. It's the breaking of the bread that makes all the difference. Before something ordinary can become extraordinary, it must first be broken. The break can make transformation happen.

> The times when God changed me the most were preceded by seasons of brokenness. The hardest part of a journey comes just before you reach the beautiful peak.
>
> —Sarah

We disciples tend to focus almost exclusively on the take and the give. We savor the way Jesus lovingly, graciously takes us into his hands for salvation. And we celebrate the way he powerfully gives us to the world for service. We are saved to serve for sure. But while the taking and the giving may be our favorite parts of the story, they are not the only or most important parts. The beginning and end of the story make sense only in light of the long middle section. In the middle, between the taking and the giving, is the breaking.

Between the taking of slaves out of Egypt and the planting of a nation into Canaan is the breaking in the wilderness. Between the taking of ordinary fishermen and the giving of apostolic leaders is the breaking that comes from the crucifixion of power-hungry dreams and warped messianic expectations. And Christ takes ordinary people like us into his hands for salvation so that he can give us, through mission, to the world. But to make the most of the take and the give, he must break us. Jesus took the ordinary bread and gave it as his extraordinary body after, and only after, the bread was broken. Transformation can happen only to what is first broken.

The implicit punch line that Christ laid on the apostles back then and lays on us today is, "Just as my hands transform the meaning of this flat, tasteless bread into something as extraordinary as my presence simply by breaking it, so will I transform you if you yield yourselves into my hands to be broken." We wonder if this invitation is all that inviting. We are fulfilled in the taking. We are fruitful in the giving. But we are fearful and frustrated in the breaking. Who wants that?

All of the chosen disciples experienced a period of brokenness during and shortly after Jesus' body was literally broken through crucifixion. They were broken through the death of their long-held messianic expectations. They were broken by the physical absence of Jesus. They were broken by the mirror that allowed them to see the ugliness in their souls. They were broken by the awareness of their cowardice, betrayal, denial, pride, and lust for power.

All of the disciples went through a period of brokenness. Some got better, while others became bitter. Judas turned on Jesus for thirty pieces of silver and was broken by betrayal. Brokenness made Judas bitter, not better, and he bailed on God. Peter cowardly denied Jesus, but was broken by his failures in a way that made him extraordinary in time. Brokenness makes some bitter and some better.

The process of brokenness is generally long, grueling, uncomfortable, inconvenient, inefficient, unwelcome, unglamorous, messy, stripping, humbling, and ego crushing. These are things that twenty-first-century churchians are taught to run from and resist at all costs. Almost from birth, we are influenced by popular culture to pursue the dream of convenience and comfort. Most of us are taught to chase our personal happiness at all costs, no matter whom we step on or what we become in the process. Looking good and feeling good seem more appealing than being good. This "dream" has seeped into the church. Cultural churchianity is initiated and perpetuated by this dream.

We are trained to run from brokenness as soon as we sense it creeping upon us. Everything around us screams that if we happen to find ourselves in a tough spot we should run from it, medicate it, seek a new lover, find a new job, get a new house, lease a new car, attend a new church, drink it away, sex it away, drug it away, success it away, video game it away, movie it away, ministry it away, or food it away.

The process of being broken can lead us to abandon or embrace faith. This process presents an occasion to either hate God or love him, to deny him or trust him. Brokenness can make us self-sufficient or God-dependent. It nurtures an environment for self-deception or self-awareness. There's only one way to come through a period of brokenness better and not bitter, to come through more extraordinary. We must resist the temptation to run *from* the brokenness and counterintuitively run *to* it. Resisting brokenness will also transform us, but not for the better.

Brokenness is designed for the crucifixion, not the exaltation, of the ego. When you are being broken, it will feel like God has abandoned you. Depression and loneliness will be so thick you can't see the light at the end of the tunnel. Brokenness will force you to face stuff about yourself that sickens you. A part of you, quite naturally, wants to run from this. Another part wants to run to the brokenness, despite the pain, because you sense it leads past the Band-Aids toward deeper surgical healing. So you choose brokenness over happiness. You realize that Christ's ultimate goal is not to make us happy but to make us holy, so that holiness is our happiness.

God transforms us through brokenness. If God did it to Hebrew slaves, to a ragamuffin group of fishermen and zealots, and to an ordinary loaf of bread, he can surely do it to us.

We must, like the bread, be broken by his hands. The bread didn't have a choice. We do.

> God's most effective tool in my life has been trouble. Being troubled when God's Word reveals my sins drives me to him and enables me to emerge out of the chrysalis of the old nature into the joyful new one. Being troubled when faced with the imminent death of a loved one has taught me to cling to God in the dark. Troubles force me to call on God for deliverance and wisdom.
>
> —Linda

THE BREAK CAN MAKE US

When we focus exclusively on the taking (salvation) and the giving (mission), we overlook the breaking (transformation) of the bread of our lives. When we concentrate solely on deliverance from Egypt (taking) and entry into the Promised Land (giving), we miss the beauty of the wilderness (breaking). We want incarnation and resurrection, but we need crucifixion too. We like the story's beginning and end, but it's the

69

middle that matters most. Between the taking and the giving is the breaking. And that's where disciples of true depth are developed.

I've been describing the transformation that comes from brokenness quite metaphorically because it's so complex. Yet the concept of brokenness needs to be expressed concretely. The best way to do this, I think, is by sharing my own experience. I pray that the sharing of my story reflects light on your own.

When I was twelve years old, my world came crashing down. I discovered that my dad, my hero, had battled a heroin addiction since his youth. Shortly after my shocking discovery, my mom, the glue that held our family together, suffered a nervous breakdown. She started using drugs with my dad. Two struggling addicts in one household is disastrous.

In a relatively short time, we lost everything. We lost our money. We lost our car. We lost our dignity. We lost our hope. We lost our minds. We lost our home. This last loss caused us to lose each other. When we found ourselves homeless, we each moved in with different extended family members. As I was heading into my freshman year of high school, I went to live with my aunt, my sister went to another aunt, my dad went to his mother, and my mom went to her parents. I was the kid with drug-addicted parents, whose family car was repossessed and house foreclosed. I was the kid everyone, including myself, pitied.

A nagging inferiority complex and deep insecurity spread rapidly through me like an aggressive cancer. To escape the shame and disgrace, I hit the bottle when I was thirteen. By my seventeenth birthday, I was a full-fledged alcoholic. I dropped out of high school early in my junior year. I couldn't keep a job. My life was spinning out of control. I initiated a drunken brawl where I was stabbed, nearly to death. While my friends were ambitiously pursuing college and career, I resigned myself to a meaningless and hopeless existence.

Then, out of nowhere, God found me. First, though, he found my parents. He led them to Teen Challenge, a Christ-centered recovery program. I spent a few months in the program too. The alcoholism and hopeless despair disappeared. With miraculous flair, God put my Humpty-Dumpty life and family back together again. I am still amazed, decades later, that what God did for me I could never have done for myself.

Here's where brokenness enters the story. God revealed something to me a few years ago that broke me. I realized that, although Christ saved me from my past, some residue remained stuck to my soul. I first became aware of it while writing in my prayer journal. I wrote about myself, "It seems there is still an insecure and inferior thirteen-year-old boy trapped inside this man, trying desperately to get healed and get out."

This revelation stunned me because it was true. I finally understood the origin of the depression and isolation that has wreaked havoc on me from time to time, even after I came to faith in Christ. God was leading me on a journey of brokenness that would transform me, but I wasn't sure I wanted to go.

God began showing me areas of my life in which my former self, the thirteen-year-old boy, was still doing damage. The mirror God held up exposed my trust issues. The people I trusted most when I was a boy, my parents, let me down by their addiction to drugs. At the age of thirteen, I subconsciously, but stubbornly, resolved to avoid putting myself in a position to need people. So I kept people at arm's length. I did this by serving them but refusing to let them serve me. My fearful insecurity made me self-reliant and arrogant and, therefore, void of the intimacy fostered by vulnerability and trust. The image of this man I saw in the mirror was unbearable. I was being broken.

Also through the mirror of brokenness, God showed me another way the thirteen-year-old boy was doing damage. As a teenager, I was smothered by inferiority. People seemed to think—and I agreed with them—that I was a loser whose life would not amount to a hill of beans. I was the kid most likely *not* to succeed. When I came into relationship with Christ, an ambition to do something meaningful with my life surfaced in me. That ambition was pure for the most part.

But there is a very thin line between holy aspiration and selfish ambition. At times I crossed that line. I entered into pastoral ministry to glorify God, to build his kingdom. But in the mirror, I realized that the driving force behind my fruitfulness in ministry was not always to glorify God, but to prove myself. I used ministry as a means to overcome my inferiority. Yet no matter how successful I was in ministry, my inferiority complex did not diminish. Ministerial success, on my worst days, became a cover for the deep insecurity, inferiority, and inadequacy I had felt and fed since the age of thirteen.

> Through the trials I have experienced, including miscarriages, a job loss, dealing with an extremely strong-willed child, caring for my sick mom, and watching my grandmother die, my loving commitment to Christ has deepened. My faith and prayer life have deepened also. I was not thankful for any one of these trials when I went through them. But because those times of brokenness brought me deeper into prayer and Scripture and opened my eyes to his awesome work, those trials are now some of my sweetest memories.
>
> —Erica

I was disgusted by the image in the mirror. It broke me. The temptation to run from brokenness was strong, but the grace to be transformed by it was even stronger.

Running to—not from—the process of brokenness that transforms us required several things from me. It required brutal reflective honesty regarding my actions and words. Do I do what I do and say what I say to prove myself and impress people or to glorify God and love people? The process also necessitated my willingness to confess my struggles to others, to trust people completely. The brokenness was healing and releasing the thirteen-year-old boy once trapped inside of me.

God is still transforming the ordinary bread of my life into something extraordinary. He still breaks me to make me what he created me to be.

BREAKING BEAUTIFUL

The Last Supper was the first celebration of the sacrament of Communion. As already mentioned, Mark's gospel reveals that the Last Supper took place during the Jewish feast of Passover. Jews had to remove every trace of yeast from their homes before Passover. Many Jewish families to this day walk around their homes with a flashlight in hand to locate and remove bread crumbs from countertops and floors before the feast.

There are various reasons for the removal of yeast, or leaven. One of them relates to transformation. Egypt, oppressor of God's people and the location of the first Passover, was likely the first place where yeast was used to make food and drink.[2] God took his people out of Egypt, but he had to find a way to take Egypt out of them. Removing yeast from the home reminded the Jews that they were to be different from the Egyptians, to be holy as God is holy. Yeast represented corruption, the sinful betrayal of the will and ways of God. God called his people "to put away all the leaven of their Egyptian nature."[3] Because of his love for us, God will expose our yeast. He does this not to shame us but to remove yeast from our lives.

That's what the process of brokenness looks like. God walks through the houses of our lives with his flashlight. He is determined to locate and remove the yeast of lust, pride, selfish ambition, haphazard spirituality, envy, arrogance, egotism, racism, sexism, consumerism, and any other "-ism" he finds in us. He does this not to hurt us but to heal us. What yeast taints the house of your life and must be removed to experience true depth in discipleship?

The Bible provides another powerful picture of the transformation that can result from brokenness. The prophet Malachi described God as a "refiner's fire" (3:2). The refiner of silver used heat to remove impurities. As part of the process, he melted the silver. The fire had to be hot enough to force the impurities to the surface where they could be skimmed off the silver. But if the fire was too hot, it could destroy the silver.

God, the cosmic refiner, turns up the heat on the silver of our lives through brokenness. The fire is not hot enough to destroy us, but it is hot enough to bring the impurities in our lives to the surface of our souls. He intends to skim off the impurities so that the silver of our lives transforms into something more extraordinary. He breaks us to transform us.

God breaks us into a million pieces in a million ways. He puts us in relationships with people we don't like but must learn to love. He ends relationships that we've turned into idols. He throws us into the fire through tasks that test our humility. He turns up the heat to expose the sins of egotism and prejudice. God draws the impurities to the surface to be skimmed. He raises the heat to refine the metal of our lives.

> I take the tough seasons of life in stride and keep moving. I have had a couple of very deep hurts. But I've tried to turn those over to the Lord to do with as he wills and to heal those areas of my heart that hurt most.
>
> —Wenda

He does this so that the silver of humanity shines again with the image of God that marked us in the garden of Eden.

Broken bread is messy. Lots of crumbs fall all over the place when we break bread. Just ask the person in your church who cleans up after Communion. This process of transforming the ordinary into something extraordinary through breaking is downright messy. Broken bread will never be the same again. You can't glue it back together. Pieces have fallen off. Flakes have come undone. The constitution of the bread is forever changed.

When Christ's hands break the loaf of our lives, crumbs fall off everywhere. The crumbs that fall off are the ones we need to shed most. Those scraps weigh us down. They smother and stifle the image of God in us. If we can find the grace to yield ourselves to the hands of Christ to be broken, the crumbs that need to fall off will do so.

You're better than ground beef. If ordinary ground beef in the hands of my wife can become the most extraordinary meat loaf that ever graced my taste buds, imagine what the hands of Christ can do with ordinary folks like us. Unlike the bread, we choose to be broken by Christ's hands. Disciples of true depth trust Christ not only to take us and give us, but also to break us in the most extraordinary ways!

SWIMMING PRINCIPLE

God breaks ordinary people to transform them into something extraordinary.

SWIMMING PRACTICE

When comparing the brokenness of biblical Christianity with the happiness of cultural churchianity, why do we have a hard time seeing the beauty and benefits of brokenness? What can the church do to confront these trends that challenge true depth discipleship?

Can you recall people from the Bible who went through a season of brokenness? Did they come through the process better or bitter? In what ways do you think God was trying to transform them?

Reflect on a period of brokenness you have experienced. How did God use it to transform you into something more extraordinary than you were before the season of brokenness?

Pray for someone you know who is in a season of brokenness.

SWIMMER'S PRAYER

Lord, we yield to your strong and loving hands so that our ordinary is transformed into extraordinary. Help us not to run from but to the seasons of brokenness that ultimately make us what you have determined we can become. Expose our sin so that you skim it off the silver of our lives and make us shine. We recognize that the most beautiful work you do is not only for us in the taking or through us in the giving, but also to us in the breaking. Amen.

NOTES

1. Frederick Buechner, *Telling the Truth: The Gospel as Tragedy, Comedy, and Fairy Tale* (San Francisco: Harper & Row, 1977), 78.

2. David Kraemer, "Leavened or Unleavened: A History," *The Jewish Daily Forward*, March 30, 2007, accessed December 3, 2014, http://forward.com/articles/10411/leavened-or-unleavened-a-history/.

3. C. F. Keil and F. Delitzsch, *Commentary on the Old Testament in Ten Volumes*, vol. 1, *The Pentateuch* (Grand Rapids, MI: Eerdmans, 1973), 21.

SANCTIFICATION
WHAT GOD DOES IN US

5

Jacob thought he was marrying one person. He got two. He served his uncle Laban for seven years. Jacob did this in exchange for Laban's beautiful daughter Rachel. Laban promised that after the seven years of service were completed, he would give Rachel to Jacob. But Laban pulled a fast one. He tricked Jacob in much the same way that Jacob had deceived everyone around him. Laban pulled a Jacob on Jacob. Instead of giving radiant Rachel, as he promised, Laban gave lackluster Leah to Jacob. In the end, Jacob got both women. He married the Rachel he wanted *and* the Leah he didn't want. This odd story can be found in Genesis 29:14–30.

If you are a married, you know what it's like to be Jacob. When you said "I do," you got the radiant "Rachel" you wanted. You married a Rachel who celebrates your greatest joys and shares your deepest sorrows, who loves you when no one else does, who services your car by changing the oil and installing snow tires, who offers physical warmth and affection, who makes you hot soup when you have a cold, who plans special getaways on your anniversary and birthday, and who puts presents under your pillow for no reason. You married a Rachel who convinces you that you are more valuable than you feel at the moment, who looks spectacular not to impress anyone else in the room but you. A Rachel who sends you two dozen roses at work just because, who brags about you to your mother-in-law. When you said "I do," you got the Rachel you wanted.

But like Jacob, when you said "I do," you got not only the radiant Rachel you wanted, but also the lackluster Leah you didn't want. You got a Leah who doesn't always embrace your inspired ideas. A Leah who leaves the toilet seat up so that you fall in during the dark of night, who uses your razor, who gives you the silent treatment and then turns to scream in your face. A Leah who spends too much money on things that don't matter to you, who complains about you to your mother-in-law, who likes music you don't like and doesn't like music you do like. A Leah who forces you to dine at a steakhouse when you are in the mood for take-out Chinese food, who has a different parenting strategy from yours. A Leah who drives you nuts at times, makes you mad on occasion, and utterly confounds you on most days.

I make it my business to share with engaged couples this little ditty, "When you say 'I do,' you're getting two." If you've been married for more than a month, you know what I'm talking about. Most couples eventually realize that Rachel and Leah live in their spouse. Upon this realization, many couples end up coexisting or quitting the marriage. There are, however, those rare couples who learn to love not only the Rachel, but also the Leah in their spouse. Their marriage is golden, a thing of beauty!

Whether or not you are married, if you are a part of the church of Jesus Christ, you know what it's like to be Jacob. When you said "I do" to God, you got the radiant Rachel you wanted. You got the Christ, a Rachel who forgives your sins, heals your wounds, lifts you out of the slimy pit, and places your feet on solid ground. You got a Rachel who says "Come to me" and readily receives you. You embraced a radiant Rachel, who keeps the promise to never reject or leave you, who breaks the bars of your sin and shame, causing you to walk with your head held high through the dignity of discipleship. You received a Rachel whose love gets you out of bed in the morning, whose presence gives you peace in the dark of the night.

This Rachel gives you wisdom and purpose you can't find anywhere else. Your Rachel finds ways to breathe life into the deflated sails of your soul. When you said "I do" to God, you got the radiant Rachel you wanted. You got Christ!

But when you said "I do" to God, you got not only the radiant Rachel, the Christ, you wanted, but you also got the lackluster Leah, the church, you didn't want. The church is a Leah that will disappoint you almost constantly. It has leaders who run off with their secretary or embezzle funds for a time-share in Hawaii. It is a Leah that fights and backbites, seems full of gossip rather than goodness, and appears more sinful than sanctified. It is full of quirky people you would never choose to spend time with if you had a choice.

I resented the church members because they didn't seem to appreciate all I was doing. They didn't help me as I wished they would. I resented people who dressed too modestly and wondered who they thought they were, being so spiritual. Then I looked at people who tended to be the opposite and wondered how they could profess to be Christians.

—Alice

It seems to major in the minors and minor in the majors. It is too racist, too sexist, too greedy, too traditional, too contemporary, too Republican, too Democrat, too restrictive, too progressive, too simplistic, or too intellectual. It sings songs you don't like and performs archaic rituals you don't get. The church is a Leah that often rubs you the wrong way.

When we said "I do" to God, we got the Christ and the church, a Leah that makes us wonder if getting Rachel is worth enduring Leah.

Let's be honest. It feels a lot like God pulled a Laban on us Jacobs! Most of us come into relationship with God expecting only Rachel; and we get lots of Rachel. But we get just as much Leah. Who in their right mind would say "I do" to the mess and the risk,

81

the failures, foibles, and flaws that constitute this Leah we call the church?

Now I caution engaged couples and new converts up front. I tell them, "When you say, 'I do,' you're getting two. You get the Rachel you want *and* the Leah you don't want."

QUITTING AND COEXISTING

Those first disciples realized that when they said "I do" to God, they got two. They got the radiant Rachel/Christ, they wanted. They also got the less-than-lovely Leah/church they didn't want. They, too, got two. Here's how Mark recorded it:

> Jesus went up on a mountainside and called to him those he wanted, and they came to him. He appointed twelve that they might be with him and that he might send them out to preach and to have authority to drive out demons. These are the twelve he appointed: Simon (to whom he gave the name Peter), James son of Zebedee and his brother John (to them he gave the name Boanerges, which means "sons of thunder"), Andrew, Philip, Bartholomew, Matthew, Thomas, James son of Alphaeus, Thaddaeus, Simon the Zealot and Judas Iscariot, who betrayed him. (Mark 3:13–19)

I have often misinterpreted the focus of this passage. I have understood it as a call to spend time *alone* with Jesus. Jesus calls me to be with him. That's an erroneous interpretation of this Scripture.

The passage above is not a call to personal relationship with Christ, but to communal relationship with him.

Look at Mark 3:14 again. Jesus designated "them" so that "they" might commune with him. Jesus sent "them" out to preach. Mark's pronouns are not singular but plural. Jesus called the Twelve to love and serve him in community not in isolation. That's why Mark took the time to list the names of the twelve men Jesus called into community. Mark named them all, even pointing out details that show Jesus chose quite a motley crew. That's where the Leah comes in.

Although the twelve men Jesus picked were all Jewish, they were rather diverse. There was Simon the Zealot. As a Jewish zealot, Simon hated anyone or anything that reeked of Rome. Someone like Simon would never normally choose to follow Jesus with Matthew the tax collector. Jewish tax collectors like Matthew were notorious for robbing their own people in the name of the Roman government and to line their own pockets. Zealots hated tax collectors. I suspect that Matthew, during his three-year journey with Jesus and the rest of the Twelve, slept very close to Jesus and kept one eye open at all times.

This tension typifies what we find from other places in the Gospels. This motley community often was not a peaceful one. The apostles argued about everything, especially about which of them was the greatest. They were jealous of each other. They tried to outdo each other. What is so strange is these twelve guys not only left everything to follow Jesus, but they also left everything to follow Jesus in a community they would never choose if they could pick.

Being with Jesus has its own obstacles. The most challenging obstacle, though, is following Jesus in community with people we don't prefer and who seem intolerable. Which one of us Jacobs would embrace community with Leah? Those first apostles may have initially thought, "Cool, I get to follow Jesus." Later, however, they realized that they got Jesus *and* a community that was frightening and frustrating. This community included Judas, the master manipulator; Matthew, the tax-collecting traitor; Peter, the know-it-all with an answer for everything; Simon the Zealot, who was always looking for a fight; and James and John, those Sons of Thunder who were often more competitive than cooperative. Leave everything to follow Jesus with them? Really?

Discipleship in the context of community is messy. If you want to enjoy eating sausage, don't watch it being made. If you get up close and personal to the sausage being made, the stench will get in your hair. The meat will get in your fingernails. The process of making sausages will probably gross you out. Sausage making is messy!

Disciple making is messy too. If you want to enjoy the church, don't watch disciples being made in community. It's hard. It's uncomfortable. It's painstaking. It's long. If you get up close and personal to disciples being made, the mess can get on you, maybe even in you. Many who struggle the most with Leah/church have seen and engaged in the making of discipleship sausage. They are lay leaders and pastors, people who have given blood, sweat, and tears to Leah. Many of them conclude that the only way to be happy is to keep the church at arm's length. Tolerate Leah as Jacob did, because if you really love Leah, she will drive you absolutely crazy.

> My church is experiencing growing pains and people are falling through the cracks. It has become a source of resentment for me, considering my past issues with the church.
>
> —Deb

The more we care about Leah, the more she will disappoint us. The more she disappoints us, the more we will be tempted to coexist with or quit her!

I have been on the verge of quitting the church, divorcing Leah, on several occasions during my tenure as a pastor. I saw and engaged in the making of discipleship sausage, and it was repulsive at times. Maybe you have had moments when you thought of divorcing Leah. You had a close encounter with a Leah who publically and passionately displayed love for God during congregational singing but was later arrested for child abuse. You saw Leahs who were quick to challenge people with memorized Bible verses, but slow to personally embody those verses. You got glimpses of sausage being made in a community that is sometimes contentious, cantankerous, and callous. You were tempted to quit the church and never return. I think I know how you feel. But since I'm writing this book and you're reading it, it seems neither of us has quit.

Quitting the church is not the most prevalent escape from true depth. Coexistence is. Most Christians would never seriously think of divorcing Leah, quitting the church. Many just settle for a marriage of coexistence. They pay the bills with Leah. They share the household chores with Leah. They raise the kids with Leah. But there's no intimacy with Leah. They may share a passing peck on the cheek, but that's it. Deep-end discipleship simply cannot occur in a marriage of coexistence with the church.

I have a friend who is caught in coexistence. He gave decades of his best energy to Leah. He invested the best of his time, talent, and treasure in the local church. At several points in the marriage, Leah burned him. She disappointed him. She didn't appreciate him. She didn't live up to his standards. So he slipped into a marriage of coexistence. He still attends church services. He sneaks in late, during opening songs, and leaves early, just before the closing benediction. He doesn't want to rub elbows with a bunch of Leahs. He shares the bills and chores with Leah, but there's no intimacy. He tolerates Leah, but critiques her harshly. Disgruntlement with Leah has made him less like radiant Rachel and more like lackluster Leah.

> When someone does something that upsets you, the unpleasant feelings you have don't stop when you leave that person's presence. Those feelings can adversely impact every relationship you have, even your walk with God.
>
> —John

There are many people whose marriage to Leah/church is marked by coexistence. They haven't physically left, but they have internally checked out. They have been offended, hurt, burned, disappointed, dismayed, discouraged, and disillusioned. Deep in the bowels of their soul, where only God can see, they have thrown up their hands and said, "I'm done loving and will simply tolerate Leah." Who can blame them?

Do you find yourself in a marriage of coexistence with the church? Do you wonder if getting Rachel is worth enduring Leah? Like it or not, when we say "I do" to God, we get the radiant Christ we want and lackluster church we don't want. They are a package deal.

NOT JACOB, BUT JESUS

Who in their right mind would want to marry Leah? Jacob didn't, but Jesus did. One day Jesus Christ, the groom, stood at the altar waiting for us to come to him. As we made our entry, the musicians didn't play, "Here comes the bride all dressed in white," but "Here comes the sinner all dressed in shame." None of us comes to Jesus looking like Rachel. We all come as Leah. We walk down the center aisle sporting a torn dress, evidence of a really bad hair day, and running mascara. We bear the baggage of our sin, shame, and struggle. Our heavenly Father arranged this marriage to his Son and paid the dowry with Christ's blood.

Jesus, unlike Jacob, knew exactly what he was getting when he wed himself to Leahs like us. If I were Jesus, I would have done what my friend's fiancée did to him. On the night of the wedding rehearsal, the day before the big day, she went AWOL. She didn't show up. No one could find her—because she didn't want to be found. Maybe she discovered a little too much Leah in my friend and therefore couldn't go through with the wedding. "But God demonstrates his own love for us in this: While we were still sinners, Christ died for us" (Rom. 5:8). While we were still Leahs, Christ wed himself to us. And he did so with joy!

Jesus knew that he was getting two when he said "I do" to each of us. He was getting a potential-infused Rachel and a problem-infested Leah. He also hoped that his love for us Leahs would bring out the radiant Rachel that God placed within us. The unconditional and unmerited love of Christ for less-than-lovely Leah, the church, makes it radiant like Rachel.

When Leah is loved and loved well, despite all of the reasons not to love her, it has a beautifying effect upon her. The apostle Paul would agree. He wrote, "Husbands, love your wives, just as Christ loved the church and gave himself up for her to make her holy, cleansing her by the washing with water through the word, and to

87

present her to himself as a radiant church, without stain or wrinkle or any other blemish, but holy and blameless" (Eph. 5:25–27). Jesus' love for Leah makes her "radiant" like Rachel!

I wish the church were more like Rachel than Leah. But tolerating the church, criticizing it, rejecting it, and hating it will not change it. Loving this Leah will. And here's the punch line: Learning to love Leah will not only bring out the Rachel in her, it will also bring out the Rachel hidden in us, too. I am not as Rachel as I hope to be, but I am more radiant than I would be because I'm in a position to learn to love, and not merely tolerate, Leah/church.

This is how God sanctifies us. Marriage is a sanctifying grace. It is the hammer God uses to chisel Leahs like us into Rachels. Marriage to the church is a premier tool God uses to sanctify the human soul. Personal Bible study and prayer are soul-sanctifying tools as well. However, Christian community is where the rubber of biblical application and prayerful submission meets the road.

Some of the most gracious people in the world are found in the church. Some cruel people are found in the church also. The hardest thing about being a Christian, let's face it, is the church. We then tend to think of the church not as a grace, but as a curse. In the church, you don't get to pick who comes. You are forced to bump up against broken people like you who have annoying idiosyncrasies. And this is precisely what makes the church such a sanctifying grace. In the process of learning to love people we don't like and putting up with the good, bad, and ugly parts of Christian community, our sanctification is accelerated.

Sanctification happens in the messiness of community. Sanctification happens when we love Leah despite her failures and flaws.

When we love lackluster Leah, there will be less Leah in each of us and, therefore, more Rachel in the church. Do you see the sanctification cycle? "Let us . . . not [give] up meeting together, as some are in the habit of doing" (Heb. 10:24–25). If we do, we will miss out on the sanctifying grace of Christian community.

The community to which Christ calls us is frightening and frustrating but formative. When we begin to follow Jesus, we not only enter into a perfect community with Father, Son, and Spirit (Rachel), we enter into an imperfect community full of broken people (Leah). Some of these Leahs think differently than I do about theology, politics, and music. Some differ from me economically, educationally, and ethnically. It's not the similarities but the differences that form me most.

Christian community would be so much easier if I could pick my own church. You know, do a house church. I would invite twelve guys who are a lot like me. They would be white, middle class, and educated. They would enjoy fly-fishing, cheer for the Philadelphia Eagles, and think my thoughts about God. They would embrace my culinary likes and dislikes. Ah, if only a church like this existed. I can almost hear Louie Armstrong singing "What a Wonderful World."

A church full of people who look, think, and live like me would do very little to develop me into a disciple of true depth. Don't get me wrong. I appreciate those friends with whom I have lots in common.

I know people love to complain about what a disappointment the church is; it's easy to do. But the church has always been there for me when I needed comfort and encouragement. There have always been people on fire for God who challenged me to explore a deeper relationship with God. There have always been people who have disappointed me, as well, which forces me to wrestle with my own hypocrisy. Either way, there has always been space for me to grow in the church.

—Sarah

But living in community with people I would not choose meets my most significant discipleship needs. It puts me on the cutting edge of spiritual formation.

Christian community is frightening and frustrating, but formative. It's that old guy who scowls at your kids because they're whispering during the sermon. It's that teenage girl who sits two pews in front of you and surfs the Internet on her phone throughout the service. It's the busybody who won't stop gossiping about people through the prayer chain. It's the pastor who makes decisions about the worship service that fly in the face of your preferences. It's that senior citizen who implies you're too young to have any wisdom. It's that young adult who suggests you're old and out of touch. It's that guy who loves the Southern gospel music that nauseates you. It's the electric guitarist on the worship team who seems more bent on showcasing her talent than glorifying God.

We naturally want to run from a community like this. I know I do. Then I realize that I am who I am because of who they are. They are a sanctifying grace to me, and to you. Christ has called us into a community we would never choose, full of violent zealots, egotistical Sons of Thunder, odorous fishermen, and a greedy tax collector. God knows that it's not the smooth edges of the church that chisel off the rough edges in us; it's the rough edges of the church that file us smooth.

Dietrich Bonhoeffer was a pastor and theologian who served in Germany during Hitler's Nazi regime. Bonhoeffer wrote a classic book called *Life Together* on how to survive church—how to love Leah and live to tell about it. The context for the book is a German church that was selling out to the nationalistic dream of Hitler's

Nazism. Some of Bonhoeffer's closest friends, local church pastors, were buying into German propaganda. They, like Hitler, began preaching a Nazi gospel instead of the Christian gospel. They were more interested in preaching German ideals than Christian values. They were caught up in the cultural churchianity of Germany.

Bonhoeffer had every reason to give up on Leah, but he did not. Instead of giving people a license to reject Leah, he wrote, "Every human wish dream that is injected into the Christian community is a hindrance to genuine community and must be banished if genuine community is to survive. He who loves his dream of a community more than the Christian community itself becomes a destroyer of the latter, even though his personal intentions may be ever so honest and earnest and sacrificial."[1] Bonhoeffer asserted that when we hold on more tightly to our ideal community than we do the real community, we can never experience the joy of the latter.

At times I am tempted to abandon the church. I have good reason for this, I think. Sometimes the political conceptions of churchianity appear to drive the church more than the theological convictions of Christianity. Cultural churchianity and biblical christianity have so little in common that attempts to syncretize the two is detestable to me. I am tempted to quit or complain about the church when I observe this. Then God reminds me that I got two when I said "I do"—the Rachel I wanted and the Leah I didn't want. I must learn to love them both.

If you want to be happy in marriage, tolerate Leah as Jacob did. But if you want to be holy in marriage, love Leah as Jesus does. As mentioned earlier, God's ultimate desire is to make us holy not happy, so that holiness is our greatest happiness.

God has used his people to deepen my relationship with him. In my young adult years, I was surrounded by men and women in the church who modeled for me lives of surrender and devotion to God through commitment and service. Many of these individuals shaped my life by identifying the gifts God placed in me. They assisted me in recognizing God's call upon my life to ministry. God continues to use the church to deepen my love for him. When we worship with one another, serve alongside of one another, and simply live life with one another, I learn more about God's creative nature and his desire to restore all creation unto himself.

—Emily

Leah, though lackluster at times, does have more than a few redeeming qualities. The church possesses more beauty than meets the eye. If it weren't for the saints I've encountered in Christian community, I'm not sure where I would be today. The problem I'm seeking to remedy is that many of us come into the church with a sky-high bar of expectation. We anticipate that the church will be all Rachel and no Leah. Then we discover that there is at least as much Leah as Rachel in the church. This throws many of us into a downward spiral of disillusionment from which some never recover. Yet it's our willingness to anticipate and accept not only the good, but also the bad and ugly experiences in the church that leads to our sanctification. I want to affirm the many reasons we have to love the church, while admitting the realities that challenge our love.

Here is one of the premier benefits of loving Leah despite all of the reasons not to: When we love lackluster Leah (church), we get to experience intimate union with radiant Rachel (Christ). Put another way, the more we give to the church, the more we get of Christ. We can't keep the church at arm's length and expect intimacy with Christ. Many have tried and failed! If we want to experience Rachel, we must love Leah too. There is a direct relationship between my level of love for the church and my level of intimacy with Christ. This makes complete sense. If you want an intimate friendship with me but constantly criticize my wife, forget about it! "Christ loved the church and gave himself up for her" (Eph. 5:25). If you are starving for more of Christ, try loving what he loves. Love the church.

RENEWAL OF VOWS

My wife dragged me to an arts and crafts festival in Kentucky. I didn't want to go. She made me go. There were thousands of peculiar people at this event who seemed to love artsy artifacts as much as she did. I was outnumbered. I pouted.

Then I saw it. It was the most unusual vase I had ever seen. The vase was made of hundreds of broken pieces of pottery from various vessels. The artist connected all of the fragments to form something whole, something beautiful. If the broken pieces stood alone, they wouldn't have been attractive at all. But there was something striking about a number of broken pieces joined together as one.

I was drawn closer to the vase, close enough to see the title. The artist called this fascinating work of art "The Body." I had my hunches, but wanted to make sure he was thinking what I was thinking. I asked, "By 'The Body' are you alluding to the apostle Paul's analogy for the church?" He replied with a smile, "Yep."

When broken people are brought together in Christ, they make something whole, something radiant. It is by being in community with Father, Son, and Holy Spirit—and with each other—that broken pieces like us become whole again. When it happens, less-than-lovely Leah becomes radiant like Rachel.

93

Paul was right when he wrote, "But we have this treasure [Christ/Rachel] in jars of clay [church/Leah] to show that this all-surpassing power is from God and not from us" (2 Cor. 4:7). God considers the church a risk worth taking. The church is more of a risk for God than it will ever be for us. Take the risk. Tie the knot. Say "I do." Your sanctification is at stake.

After ten years of marriage, Amy and I renewed our wedding vows. We were not expecting the vow renewal ceremony to be nearly as meaningful as our wedding ceremony, but it was.

The vow renewal ceremony meant as much to us as the ceremony on our wedding day, perhaps more. Here's why: When we said "I do" on our wedding day, we assumed we were getting only the Rachel we wanted. That was an easy "I do." After ten years of marriage, however, we understood that we got two when we said "I do," the Rachel we wanted and the Leah we didn't want. To look into each other's eyes after ten years of marriage and say "I do"—now that was special. We essentially were saying, "For better or worse, in health and sickness, I take not only the Rachel, but also the Leah in you." This kind of unconditional love and commitment, in time, remediates the Leah and radiates the Rachel in marriage.

You know now what you may not have known when you wed yourself to Christ. When you said "I do," you got two. You got Christ *and* the church, beauty *and* the beast, Rachel *and* Leah, the treasure *and* the jar of clay. Would you still say "I do" to God, knowing what you know now about the church? I hope so. Again, your sanctification is at stake.

If you're ready, let's renew our vows.

Do you vow to love the church despite its failures, foibles, and flaws, so that your love for it makes you and it more radiant?

If so, say, "I do."

Do you vow to resist the urge to carelessly coexist with or callously quit the church when it drives you crazy, because it will?

If so, say, "I do."

Do you vow to give when you want to withhold, show up when you want to stay home, serve when you'd rather not, reconcile when you'd rather avoid, and commend the church more than you critique it?

If so, say, "I do."

Do you vow to live as if the ultimate hope for the world is not the Republican Party, Democratic Party, or Tea Party, not MSNBC, FOX, or CNN, but Christ through the church?

If so, say, "I do."

Do you vow to recognize that you need the church at least as much as it needs you if you are ever going to experience deep union with Christ and become the radiant Rachel he created you to be?

If so, say, "I do."

Do you vow to love the Christian community, a Leah that is frightening and frustrating but formative?

If so, say, "I do."

SWIMMING PRINCIPLE

God uses the local church community that is frightening and frustrating but formative to perform a work of sanctification in us.

SWIMMING PRACTICE

How do you reconcile the conflicts between Christ and the church?

How has learning to love the church, despite all of the reasons not to love it, sanctified your soul?

What glimpses of beauty do you see in the church?

What are one or two ways that God can use you to make your local church less like lackluster Leah and more like radiant Rachel?

SWIMMER'S PRAYER

Lord, please cultivate in us a love for the church that matches your love for it. Even and especially when the church reveals its ugliness, help us to love it in a way that sanctifies it and us. Use the frightening and frustrating local church to form us. When we are tempted to quit or coexist with the church, remind us that "Christ loved the church and gave himself up for her." Lord, if you, the perfect one, can love the imperfect church, who are we not to do the same? Amen.

NOTE

1. Dietrich Bonhoeffer, *Life Together*, trans. John W. Doberstein (San Francisco: Harper & Row, 1954), 27.

MISSION
WHAT GOD DOES THROUGH US

6

More than 75 percent of students have been bullied verbally, mentally, or physically. An estimated 160,000 students miss school daily because they are bullied or fearful of being bullied. Every seven minutes a child is bullied on the playground.[1] Bullied students experience an increased risk of anxiety, sleep difficulties, and poor school adjustment. There is a strong association between bullying and suicide-related behaviors, including depression and delinquency.[2]

Bullying is a big problem today. It has always been a problem. About halfway through the gospel of Mark, we read that Jesus embarked on a journey to Jerusalem to face some big bad bullies. That's what his Father asked him to do. Jesus didn't want to disappoint his Dad.

I remember the time my father asked me to face a big bad bully. I grew up in South Philadelphia. Philly is the home of Rocky Balboa, excellent pizza, exquisite soft pretzels, greasy-good cheesesteaks, and, unfortunately, more bullies per capita than any other city in the world. I can't prove it, but I know it's true.

When I was ten years old, Mike was the notorious neighborhood bully. One day Mike terrorized my older sister. This was fine with me, but not with my dad. When my dad came home from work, my sister told him all of the nasty names Mike called her, names I can't repeat. After dinner Dad called me over to the living room sofa. He said, "Son, put on your sneakers, go knock on Mike's door, and tell him to meet you on the corner of Camac Street for a fight." I wasn't raised in a Christian home and certainly won't endorse violence at all with my kids. But this was my reality at the time.

I didn't want to do it. Mike was too big, too strong, and too tough for me. I had the choice of disobeying and disappointing my dad or facing the bully. As a ten-year-old boy, I still cared about pleasing my dad. He was my hero. So I decided to face the bully.

I reluctantly began the journey to Mike's house because that's what my dad asked me to do. The walk felt like a mile. It was only thirty yards. My heart was pounding out of my chest. I hoped to pass out and get rushed to the hospital. That didn't happen. All I wanted to do after dinner was play my Atari video game system. I wanted to play Frogger. Now I was the frog that was going to get crushed!

I knocked on Mike's door. He answered with grease, probably from a cheesesteak, dripping down his rocklike chin. I said, "Mike, umm, how's it goin'?" He grunted his greeting. I tentatively continued, "My dad wants me to fight you on the corner of Camac Street for bullying my sister." Mike got a sparkle in his eyes and said, "I'll be right there."

Shoot! I had hoped he would decline the invitation.

I headed toward the corner of Camac Street, where the fight with the neighborhood bully was about to go down. Why would my father put me through this discomfort? Why would my dad call me to go to a place I didn't want to go? You will read the rest of this story later. For now, it's important to know one thing: The only reason I went to face the bully was because my dad asked me to go. I didn't want to disappoint my dad.

Jesus went to an uncomfortable place, to face bullies in Jerusalem. He went because that's what his Father asked him to do. Jesus didn't want to disappoint his Dad.

Jesus was in the shire of safe predictability when the call came. You *Lord of the Rings* fans know that the "shire" is a symbol of safe predictability and status quo. It's a protective bubble that lacks adventure. But it's perfect for risk-averse people.

Well, Jesus was in the shire of Capernaum when he was called to face the bullies. He was growing in power and popularity in the region. His ministry was headquartered in Capernaum, a small and rural fishing village. Jesus was well-known and, for the most part, well liked in that small town. He could have gotten himself elected to power. He could have made a decent living. He could have experienced the ancient Near Eastern dream—a three-bedroom dirt-and-straw house with 2.2 donkeys. Jesus could have capitalized on his ministry's momentum to fuel his comfort, coziness, and convenience in Capernaum. Jesus could have lived "the good life." Just when things were looking up for Jesus, he made a dangerous decision.

> They were on their way up to Jerusalem, with Jesus leading the way, and the disciples were astonished, while those who followed were afraid. Again he took the Twelve aside and told them what was going to happen to him. "We are going up to Jerusalem," he said, "and the Son of Man will be delivered over to the chief priests and teachers of the law. They will condemn him to death and will hand him over to the Gentiles, who will mock him and spit on him, flog him and kill him. Three days later he will rise." (Mark 10:32–34)

"Up to Jerusalem" is a phrase used twice in this short passage. Going to the city of Jerusalem was physically an uphill climb. For Jesus, however, going to the place the Father was calling him to go was also a spiritual and emotional uphill climb. He was going up to Jerusalem to face big bad bullies.

As they were heading up to Jerusalem, Jesus' followers were "astonished" and "afraid." Why? Was it the nearly hundred-mile journey from Capernaum to Jerusalem? Maybe they were so used to the safe shire, the rural region of Galilee, that the large, crowded city of Jerusalem seemed scary. Who knows what might happen in the big city? Maybe simply trying to keep up with Jesus was frightening.

Before I began following Christ, I had the impression that the Christian life was boring, predictable, safe, and tame. I was wrong! The truth is that the Capernaums we create *are* bland. They're safe but dull. Following Jesus, however, is an adventure. He keeps leading us out of our Capernaums, out of the safe, predictable shires we have built for ourselves. He leads us into various Jerusalems, where anything might happen, where we are not in control, where the bullies are punching their hands waiting for us to show up.

In Jerusalem Jesus wasn't crowned king. He didn't find coziness, comfort, and convenience. He was rejected, betrayed, arrested, condemned, mocked, spat upon, flogged, and killed. And he knew it would happen. Why did Jesus leave the safe shire of Capernaum? Why did he embark on a journey to Jerusalem to face bullies who would kill him? Because that's what his Father asked him to do, and he didn't want to disappoint his Dad. Jesus cared more about pleasing his Father than preserving his life.

JESUS THE BULLY BASHER

Jerusalem was a bully magnet. Jerusalem means "city of peace," a place of *shalom*. Historically, however, the city had been anything but peaceful. The city had seen more than its fair share of bloodshed and oppression. Jerusalem attracted outsider and insider bullies.

One of the big and bad outsider bullies was the Babylonian army. The Babylonians devoured just about every nation in the ancient Near East. They took control. They came against the Jews in 589 BC. God's chosen people piled inside the city of Jerusalem, hoping the fortified walls would protect them from the vicious Babylonians. It did—for a while. As the food supply was exhausted, the Jewish people resorted to cannibalism. Eventually, the Jews surrendered to the Babylonian bully, and the bully carried them off into exile in 586 BC.

During the time of Jesus, the biggest bully in Jerusalem was an insider, not an outsider. Sure, the Roman government was an outsider bully that oppressed the Jews in Jesus' day. But the Romans used people on the inside to do the actual bullying. The Jewish chief priests who controlled the temple did most of the bullying. They oppressed their own Jewish people in the Jerusalem temple, making it difficult for poor peasant Jews to worship.

Jews returned annually to the Jerusalem temple, from all over the region, to celebrate the Jewish Passover. When they did, they had to exchange their regional money for temple currency. The temple officials seized the opportunity and charged exorbitant exchange rates. It was religious robbery!

But wait! It gets worse. Those Jews who traveled a significant distance to Jerusalem for the Passover feast could not bring an animal sacrifice from home. Nope. They had to purchase their animal sacrifice for the temple in the temple. Those animals were preapproved or, more accurately, priest-approved. As you may have guessed, the priests marked up the price of animal sacrifices substantially. Although a worshiper could find a good deal on an animal sacrifice on the way to Jerusalem, he was forced to pay top dollar for a sacrifice sold in the temple.

According to Mark 11:15, "on reaching Jerusalem," Jesus didn't waste any time before going into the temple to face the bullies. "Jesus entered the temple courts and began driving out those who were buying and selling there. He overturned the tables of the money changers and the benches of those selling doves." Many of us have interpreted this text as evidence that Jesus was unhappy with buying and selling in God's house. That's not entirely on target. Jesus was not ultimately upset that people were buying and selling in the temple; he was angry that they were bullying and oppressing in the temple. So Jesus came to Jerusalem and put himself in the tight, terrifying space between the bullies and the bullied. You know where that got him.

My older sister, Tammy, attracted lots of bullies. She was, like Jerusalem, a bully magnet. One time when I was twelve years old and Tammy was thirteen, I was playing baseball with my buddies in the schoolyard and she and her friends were sitting on the steps in front of the schoolyard. All of a sudden, I heard yelling and screaming coming from my sister's location. We went to see what was happening. A fifteen-year-old named John was bullying Tammy. He forced her over the hood of a car with his left hand while grasping a beer bottle in his right hand. He was going to smash the bottle over her head.

Everyone looked at me as if to say, "Do something." But I was scared out of my sneakers. John was three years older than I, and meaner. I wasn't going to do a thing. I rationalized my cowardice. I thought, "My sister probably deserved it. . . . She had it coming. . . . My sister can be a real pain. . . . Perhaps this will humble her in a good way." Deep down I knew I should do something, but I was paralyzed by fear.

John grabbed my sister by the hair and threw her onto the ground. He walked toward her with the beer bottle still firmly in his hand. Then, out of nowhere, a quiet and unassuming kid from the neighborhood rose up to save the day. His name was P. J. He stepped in the tight and terrifying space between the bullied and the bully, between my sister and John. He walked toward John and said, with Rocky Balboa swag, "Why don't you try throwing me around?" John wisely backpedaled until he disappeared from the scene. P. J. saved the day. He made a public spectacle of John the bully.

On a larger, cosmic scale, this is what Jesus did for us in Jerusalem. He went into the temple, into the tight and terrifying space between the bullied and the bullies. Jesus could not stand by and watch. He could not stay on the safe sidelines. He could not leave well enough alone. He just couldn't mind his own business, turn a blind eye, and ignore the bullying. He put himself between the bullied and the bullies. Crucifixion was the cost. That's what bullies do to people who get in their way.

But hold on! What the bullies could never have imagined was that as they were, in their minds, walloping Jesus, he was walloping them. When Jesus went obediently to Jerusalem to suffer and die for the bullied, he "disarmed the powers and authorities, he made a public spectacle of them, triumphing over them by the cross" (Col. 2:15). The what? The cross! A battle was raging between Jesus the bully basher and some big bad bullies. The winner by a knockout and the undisputed, undefeated heavyweight champion of the world was—and is—Jesus!

The doctrine of the incarnation is a central tenet of the Christian faith. Through the incarnation, the God who says, "Come to me," comes to us. He enters the eye of humanity's most intense storm. Jesus Christ, God in the flesh, runs *to* not *from* the Jerusalem of our sin and shame, our heartache and pain. The incarnation of Jesus Christ is God's way of picking up his cosmic bullhorn and proclaiming, "I love you, the human race, so much that I can no longer stand by and watch you get bullied. I will come to you as one of you to save you because I love you. I will step into the terrifyingly tight space between you and the forces that bully you. I, the God of the universe, will take one on the chin and bite the bullet for you. The punishment for sin will be upon me, so that by my wounds you will be healed."

> I have grown in the area of empathy and love for my neighbor. The activity of mission to others has provided the medium for spiritual growth that would not have happened otherwise.
>
> —Stephen

Jesus the bully basher saved us from some big bad bullies. Can you name the bullies that were having their way with you before Jesus came into your Jerusalem and stepped in the space between you and them? We were no match for those bullies. Their names were not Mike and John, but sin, shame, regret, addiction, emptiness, loneliness, lifelessness, anxiety, fear, depression, disappointment, despair, insecurity, inadequacy, and inferiority. There was no way we could overcome these bullies on our own, no matter how many self-help books we read. Those bullies were way too big for us, but not too big for Jesus. He came near and set us free from the bullies, He made a spectacle of them, triumphing over them by the cross! This is the gospel of our Lord Jesus Christ. And we say, thanks be to God! But that's not all.

GOD CALLS US TO THE SPACE BETWEEN

Here's the rest of the gospel: What Jesus did for us, he wants to do through us. "We are therefore Christ's ambassadors, as though God were making his appeal through us" (2 Cor. 5:20). "In this world we are like Jesus" (1 John 4:17). Jesus said, "I have set you an example that you should do as I have done for you" (John 13:15). Jesus calls disciples to "go into all the world" (Mark 16:15) on a bully-bashing mission with him. Invitations from God to partner with him in doing for others what he has done for us fill the Bible. He calls us to break free from the shire of safe status quo so that we can join him in the scary space between the bullied and bullies.

We experience God's presence and power most profoundly in the center of his will. But the center of God's will is often Jerusalem, the petrifying space between the bullies and the bullied. Over and over again, the Bible asserts that the place we least want to go is frequently where we experience God's presence and power most intensely. We find fulfillment from God's presence and fruitfulness from God's power in Jerusalem, the space between. If we run from the bullies in Jerusalem, from the mission to which God calls us, we will inevitably feel lonely and lifeless.

While Jesus spent his early ministry days in cozy Capernaum, he knew his mission would take him to risky Jerusalem. When it did, he went despite the sacrifices. He left Capernaum. He went to Jerusalem. He calls us to join him there. If we rarely or never embark on an uphill journey into God's Jerusalem mission, it's not because God isn't calling us to go. It's because we're not willing to go.

Sometimes self-deception gets the best of me. I can trick myself into believing that I'm following Christ on a mission to Jerusalem, when I'm really trying to squeeze him into my comfortable Capernaum. This deceit is so subtle.

Thus a tug-of-war goes on in the disciple's soul. We keep trying to pull Jesus into our Capernaum to help build our kingdom. (That's the way of cultural churchianity.) Meanwhile Jesus is trying to pull us into Jerusalem to build God's kingdom. (That's biblical Christianity.) Jesus, of course, is strong enough to win the tug-of-war hands down. But he won't force us into his mission. The disciple ultimately decides the tug-of-war winner.

Too many people in too many churches say they don't experience God's profound presence and power. So they throw up their hands and conclude that either God doesn't exist or he has abandoned them. There's another possibility. Maybe we feel the absence of God's powerful presence because we make choice after choice in word, thought, or deed to turn back from Jerusalem and toward Capernaum, away from compassion, courage, and commitment and toward comfort, coziness, and convenience; away from the savage storm and toward the safe shire; away from biblical Christianity and toward cultural churchianity.

When you get the chance to actually speak about who God is, what he is like, and what he has done in the world and in you, it is the most energizing and faith-strengthening experience. There is nowhere that I have learned more or have been more amped up than in mission to others.

—Sarah

If we want God, we must join him where he is at work. God is in the eye of humanity's storm. He stands out on a limb of love. He dwells in the scary space between the bullies and the bullied.

If we train ourselves to repeatedly ignore God's call to Jerusalem, we will ultimately stop hearing the call altogether. That's alarming. My wife asked me to fix the sliding closet door in our bedroom for six months straight. I agreed to fix it every time she asked, but didn't budge. At first I felt guilt. But my repeated refusal to respond to my wife's call to the closet door mission diminished the guilt I felt. After a while, I learned to close my ears to her request. My wife finally went with plan B. She pulled the door off the track and put it in the garage. God will find a plan B to help the bullied, but you are his plan A.

Cultural churchianity is as boring and predictable as a Midwest cornfield. It entails no exciting adventure, just a long stretch of flatness. Biblical Christianity, however, offers a thrilling roller coaster ride. Jesus went up to Jerusalem, down to the grave, rose up after three days, ascended to heaven after forty days, and will someday come down again to be with us. Jesus doesn't stay still. If following Jesus feels stagnant, then maybe you're not following Jesus. Perhaps you're trying to get Jesus to follow you into the safe Capernaum of cultural churchianity.

It has become popular over the past few decades to make Christianity more about the Christian than Christ. Some preachers lead us to believe that our "best life now" awaits us in the safe shire of Capernaum, where cars are luxurious, houses are huge, and health prevails. Easy street! Yet Jesus and the biblical narrative keep calling us to Jerusalem, to unpredictable and unsafe places. There we find not power, popularity, prestige, and prosperity, but the profundity of God's presence, power, and plan.

It bears repeating: Cultural churchianity is founded on trying to get God to build our kingdom in Capernaum. Biblical Christianity happens when God gets us to build his kingdom in Jerusalem. Churchianity is about getting God to give us possessions, prestige, and popularity. Christianity happens when the centripetal force of the presence, power, and plan of the Trinitarian God pulls us into his mission.

Jesus does not exist to help us build our safe shires. Actually, he came to save us from our shires. Even a casual reading of the four gospels proves it. Jesus calls would-be disciples to leave their nets and boats, to sell their possessions and give the proceeds to the poor, to deny themselves and take up their cross, and to lose their life in order to find it. Disciples are called to break free from their attachments so they can join Jesus in his bully-bashing mission. That's what true depth discipleship looks like.

> At first, my desire was to work with women caught in sex-trafficking. I have since been led to speak directly to traffickers. God keeps placing me in a position to speak directly to those who buy and sell human beings as slaves.
>
> —Deb

The church of Jesus Christ has always been on a bully-bashing mission. Do you know what led in the fight against the bully of racism throughout the past centuries? The church! Do you know what took the front line in the battle to abolish the bully of slavery?

God has been using our church's food pantry to shape me as I engage in mission to others. Specifically, he uses the people receiving help from the pantry to shape me. I have the honor of praying with them while they wait in line to receive food. God uses their prayer requests to impact me. God challenges me through their requests to pray big or go home. My faith is tested as I ask him to heal diseases, provide food and shelter for a homeless man, or free a battered woman from abuse. I used to be nervous and hesitant in this mission. Not anymore. God has blessed me with a joyous opportunity to be his loving hug for a hurting world.

—Erica

The church! Do you know what first stood up to the bully of addiction by starting recovery programs? The church! Do you know what was brave enough to journey all over the world to build hospitals, schools, and orphanages in places where bullies abound? The church! Do you know what sought the equality of women by tackling the bully of sexism? The church! The church has been at its best when it has broken free from the shire to join Christ in the space between the bullies and the bullied.

Mark 10 highlights how hard it is for humans to break free from the shires we build for ourselves. In the passage just before Jesus declared his commitment to go up to Jerusalem to suffer and die for humanity at the hands of bullies (see Mark 10:32–34), a rich man refused to leave his Capernaum of possessions to follow Jesus to Jerusalem. In the passage that follows Jesus' declaration of his death mission, James and John revealed their fixation on the Capernaum of power. "Let one of us sit at your right and the other at your left in your glory" (10:37), they asked Jesus.

Jesus, the one who put himself between the bullied and the bullies, is the anomaly in between these two passages in Mark 10. Jesus stands in contrast to the rich man and the Sons of Thunder. He relinquished his possessions and power in order to squeeze himself into the space between the human race and the biggest bullies that seek to destroy us. He calls us to join him in doing for others what he has done for us.

Mark, I think with a touch of irony, pointed out in chapter 10 that the only person willing to follow Jesus to Jerusalem was a former blind guy. As soon as blind Bartimaeus received his sight, he "followed Jesus along the road" (10:52) to Jerusalem. Once Bartimaeus had eyes to see, he went in the direction Jesus was heading. Those with spiritual eyes to see will do the same.

WHAT IS YOUR JERUSALEM?

God has a track record of entering into the tight space between the bullies and the bullied; between the Egyptian oppressors and the Hebrew slaves; between Goliath-sized Philistines and the Israelite nation; and between sin, decay, and death and the human race. God not only filled the space between, but he invited Moses, David, Christ, and us to squeeze into the space with him. The question is, will we? If we do, we will discover that the Jerusalem we are tempted to run from, oddly enough, is the mission for which God made us. We have to stop waiting for God to show up in our Capernaum and instead join him in his Jerusalem, where he already is at work.

The big question that demands an answer is, to which Jerusalem is God calling you to go? Someone somewhere is being bullied. The bullied are waiting for you to show up. Will you squeeze into the space between the bullied and the bullies, between the oppressed and the corrupt systems of injustice, between a teenager and the rejection he feels, between a single mom with three kids and the bills that threaten to leave them homeless? Who will enter the space between a village of people in Africa and a lack of clean water, between an addicted friend and the alcohol that is destroying her, between ethnic minorities and racist stereotyping, between a significant mission opportunity and the lack of resources to pursue it? Will you enter the space between the struggling church member and the thin spiritual thread that's about to break, between unbelievers and their eternal separation from God, between the youth of the church and the lack of volunteers willing to serve and mentor them? Who will join Christ in the space between women and the chauvinism that oppresses them; between the poor and the challenges that suffocate them; between people who are literally bullied at work, school, and home and the bullies who torture them? Who will enter the space between right and wrong, truth and lies, hope and hopelessness, and reconciliation and rejection?

To which Jerusalem is God calling you? Go! That's where you will find God's presence and power most profoundly. Joining Jesus in mission will require a sacrificial risk of time, energy, money, reputation, safety, and comfort. But if Jesus is there—and he is—nothing else really matters. His presence and power are all that we need to be fulfilled and fruitful. The place we least want to go and the thing we least want to do may be, in fact, the situation we long for the most.

I was comfortable and cozy in my Capernaum. Then I read these words from an article in *The New York Times* that changed everything: "The findings have surfaced with ominous regularity over the last few years, and with little notice: Members of the clergy now suffer from obesity, hypertension and depression at rates higher than most Americans. In the last decade, their use of antidepressants has risen, while their life expectancy has fallen. Many would change jobs if they could. Public health experts who have led the studies caution that there is no simple explanation of why so many members of a profession once associated with rosy-cheeked longevity have become so unhealthy and unhappy."[3]

My Jerusalem these days is the space between pastors and the disappointment, depression, and demoralization that seek to devour them.

My hunch is that God is calling you to some Jerusalem, to some space between the bullied and the bullies. Perhaps he has been calling you to a particular bully-bashing mission for a few months. Or maybe he has been trying to get you to join him for many years, decades even. You offer any combination of the following excuses: "I'm too young. I'm too old. I will go when my kids are grown. I will do it when I have more time. I will go when I have the money. I'm not skilled enough. I'm afraid of losing everything. That's an impossible task. I'm afraid of failing." Don't keep putting off until tomorrow what God is calling you to tackle today. Tomorrow might not come for the bullied.

My three-year-old son and I drove through our town. At his direction, we stopped to pray with families at random houses. I tried to avoid one particularly run-down house, but my son was insistent that our prayers for them were necessary. As we spoke to a young single man named Anthony who had two children, a connection was made to a mutual friend. After we prayed and left, our mutual friend called and said he had been reaching out and inviting Anthony to church for more than a year. My son's prayer finally broke through to Anthony's heart and he agreed to attend.

—Jeff

Are you willing to face bullies that are way too big for us but not too big for God? Are you willing to go to Jerusalem and fight the bullies that are pummeling the human race, bullies that leave people broken, desperate, and afraid? Are you willing to go because of a call from the Father to go? Will you face the bullies or disappoint your Dad? Will you please your Father or preserve your shire?

GOD IS ALWAYS WHERE HE SENDS YOU

Now back to the opening story. My dad sent me to "Jerusalem" to face Mike, the toughest kid in our neighborhood. I could disappoint my dad or take a beating. I chose the latter. When I arrived at the corner of Camac Street for a showdown with the bully, guess who was already there? My dad! He was not in the house reading the newspaper, napping on the sofa, or playing Atari. He was on the corner, and in my corner, waiting for me to join him there in the space between the bullied and the bully.

Mike arrived. Something told me he would. We went toe-to-toe, for about five seconds until Mike knocked me to the ground. He jumped on top of me, throwing fast and furious punches. Dad functioned as the referee and broke us up. He also served as my trainer, you know, my very own corner guy. After separating us, Dad gave me a chance to catch my breath. He whispered, "Go get him, Son." Mike eventually knocked me to the ground again. Again, Dad broke us up and whispered, "Go get him, Son." This happened three or four times. The fight ended when Mike and I were exhausted, Mike from hitting me, and me from getting hit. Believe it or not, after the fight, my dad invited Mike over to our house to play Atari. That seems more odd to me now than it did then.

Mike stopped bullying my sister and me. It wasn't because he feared me. He feared my dad. Mike realized that he was no match for my dad. I was grateful that Dad was there on Camac Street before I even arrived to face the bully. Dad did not ask me to go where he would not be present and in my corner.

The same is true of God. Mark told his readers that the disciples were heading toward Jerusalem "with Jesus leading the way" (10:32). Jesus goes ahead of us to the place he calls us to go. He is already there, leading the way. God's mission always takes us where his grace will sustain us. He arrives in Jerusalem first. We experience the grace of God most profoundly in the space between the bullied and the bullies. God is where he calls you to go.

SWIMMING PRINCIPLE

God accomplishes his mission through us when we dare to join him in the space between the bullied and the bullies.

SWIMMING PRACTICE

Jesus entered the space between you and your bullies. What or who are those bullies Jesus bashed on your behalf?

What are some of the most powerful bullies oppressing humanity today?

Once Jesus does some bully bashing for us, he wants to do some bully bashing through us. To what space between the bullied and the bullies is Jesus calling you? What kinds of sacrifices might your going involve?

What excuses for not going with Jesus on your bully-bashing mission do you need to overcome?

SWIMMER'S PRAYER

Lord, set us free from the shires of safe predictability we have built for ourselves. We want to join you in Jerusalem. Fill our hearts so deeply with compassion for the bullied that we are miserable until we act on their behalf. We will leave our fishing boats and nets, our North American dreams, or whatever else keeps us from going where you're calling us to go and doing what you're calling us to do. We pray on behalf of the bullied and in the name of Jesus Christ, the bully basher. Amen.

NOTES

1. "Bullying Statistics, The Ultimate Guide," NoBullying.com, accessed December 5, 2014, http://nobullying.com/bullying-statistics/.

2. "Bullying Statistics," Pacer's National Bullying Prevention Center, accessed November 30, 2014, http://www.pacer.org/bullying/about/media-kit/stats.asp.

3. Paul Vitello, "Taking a Break from the Lord's Work," *The New York Times*, August 1, 2010, http://www.ny times.com/2010/08/02/ny region/02burnout.html?pagewanted=all&_r=0.

PUTTING IT ALL TOGETHER

7

I started running on a treadmill during a very stressful period in my life. My family was growing rapidly. We had three kids in just over three years. The church I pastored was growing. Conflict was growing. And my belly was growing. I gained nearly twenty pounds in one year. I could not ignore the treadmill that stood in the corner of our basement any longer. In 2006 I stepped on the treadmill and never looked back.

I exercised three times a week. My workout consisted of a three-mile run. I sweat and ached like I was running a marathon, but I stuck with it. It took me about two years to knock off the twenty pounds. Now I run seven to nine miles for each of my three or four weekly workouts. I never could have imagined back in 2006 that I would someday run eight miles in an hour on a regular basis. I run faster and farther than I ever dreamed possible.

It didn't happen overnight. I made incremental strides. I was devoted to my exercise routine. I was disciplined with my time. Only legitimate emergencies interrupted my workout schedule. I was willing to make sacrifices and experience pain in order to develop my running strength and stamina. And there was progress. In nine years, I went from running three miles in thirty-five minutes to running eight miles in sixty minutes. If I were still stuck on the three-mile distance I ran nine years ago, you would question my level of dedication.

Too many Christians start and stay at the three-mile mark in their discipleship run. They don't advance beyond where they started. Some even go backward. They start off running three miles but in a few years find they can't even reach the two-mile mark. Their dedication to Christ has not grown stronger as they've grown older.

Stagnancy is a problem. Stagnant discipleship diminishes the church's witness to the world. My conversation with a Muslim cab driver provides a case in point. I was gently bearing witness to my faith in Christ and Christ's love for him. The cabby responded, "You Christians are just like everyone else. Your faith doesn't seem to cost you anything. You want God without sacrifice." Ouch! He didn't voice this in a harsh manner. He simply offered his perspective. This man's comments confirm the plague of cultural churchianity. Stagnant and shallow discipleship destroys the church and diminishes its witness to the watching world.

Disciples who swim in the depths counter this terrible trend. They swim in deeper waters, and they run farther as they grow older in Christ. They start the first year of their relationship with Christ by running two miles on the treadmill. In five years, they run four miles. After they have followed Christ for a decade, they run seven miles. After a quarter century, they run marathons. Their run on the treadmill of the Christian journey progressively improves over time. Why? Because these growing disciples are experiencing, on a consistent basis, what we all need to run the race well—revelation, restoration, transformation, sanctification, and mission. God uses these dynamics to develop disciples of true depth.

ONE SWIMMER'S STORY

We have been exploring each of the five forces of deep discipleship in isolation so that each receives careful treatment. In actuality, however, they work in concert to form the disciple. Let's look at a snapshot of revelation, restoration, transformation, sanctification, and mission in one swimmer's story.

Dana was born and raised in Queens, New York. He did not grow up in a Christian home. By the time he hit his thirties, he was addicted to cocaine and operating an illegal gambling racket. Dana hit rock bottom. He spent time in a drug rehabilitation center, where he met his future wife and God.

REVELATION

God revealed himself to Dana in undeniable ways. Christ's loving presence was palpable. God showed up to speak up in his life through circumstances and people. Dana paused long enough to stop, look, and listen. When he did, he became more intoxicated with Christ than with crime or cocaine. Eventually, he stopped using drugs and walked away from the million-dollar gambling operation. He sensed God was leading him to move his family out of New York and into the Pocono Mountains of Pennsylvania. That's where I met him.

RESTORATION

Dana started to attend the church I served as pastor. He still was trying to overcome some guilt from his past. He needed a mulligan from God. And he got one. Dana was forgiven, and he knew it. God's grace helped Dana overcome his tendency to replay the regrettable slices of the past and recommit the sinful slices in the present. I got a front-row seat in the theater of God's restorative grace. God's grace-filled mulligan restored the *imago Dei*, the image of God, in Dana.

TRANSFORMATION

Dana was attending our church for about a year before the crimes of his past caught up to him. He'd made the mistake of maintaining communication with the young man who took over the illegal gambling operation. The police were tapping the phone lines of the bookie, and Dana was caught in the sting. He was going to prison for his involvement in an organized crime bookmaking syndicate. The months preceding his incarceration began the brokenness. Dana would show up on Sundays and weep through the entire worship service. He sat in the back of the sanctuary, but I could still hear him crying while I preached. God was holding up a mirror that exposed the compromise in Dana's life.

After the birth of his third child, Dana went to prison for a year. Prison was a painful but transformational experience for him. I spoke to him a few times while he was there. He was a wreck and struggled to maintain his sanity. He was afraid. He was depressed. He was paranoid. He was neurotic. But through it all, he clung to God with a death grip. God was crucifying Dana's ego. Prison may be the most effective venue for the kind of brokenness that leads to transformation. God transformed ordinary Dana into something more extraordinary through this process of brokenness.

SANCTIFICATION

Dana needed a job before he could be released on parole from prison. The church knew that hiring an ex-con was risky, especially since we ran a preschool. We offered him a job anyway. The congregation's willingness to embrace him despite his past and public crimes overwhelmed him. One guy from the congregation even put up the money for Dana's bail. Dana thought he was returning to a congregation that would be suspicious of him, now that we all knew about his dark past. Instead, he found a church family that loved him despite his failures and flaws. Sure, a few were cynical of Dana's prison transformation. God used both the cynics and the supporters to sanctify Dana. That congregation was sanctified too. The people became less like lackluster Leah and more like radiant Rachel as they loved Dana in spite of any reasons not to love him.

MISSION

We hired Dana out of prison to maintain the church building. We hoped he would be our fix-it guy. He was, but not in the way we anticipated. Dana was horrible at fixing things, but really skilled at fixing people. He had a passion to tell and show others what God, through Christ, has done for him. God was calling him to enter the missional space between the bullied and the bullies. Dana joined God in the space between addicts and the drugs, alcohol, and gambling that bullied them. Dana refused to play life safe by building his kingdom in Capernaum and, instead, risked his life building God's kingdom in Jerusalem among addicts. Today, he is the co-lead pastor of the congregation that embraced him. Dana and this local church have helped hundreds of addicts overcome the bully of addiction.

Dana's story is still being written by the God who reveals, restores, transforms, sanctifies, and sends on mission. I share Dana's story to give you a glimpse into how God uses the primary pieces of the discipleship puzzle to develop disciples of true depth.

SWIM THEOLOGY

Making disciples is the work of God through the local church. Although we have a significant role to play in our discipleship, God is the primary actor. Discipleship, then, is more theological than anthropological; it depends more on what God does than what we do. Many discipleship programs and books stress what we do to make disciples: We worship, fellowship, serve, grow, and reach out. However, it's not ultimately what we do for God but what God does among, for, to, in, and through us that cultivates true depth. God makes disciples. He always has and always will.

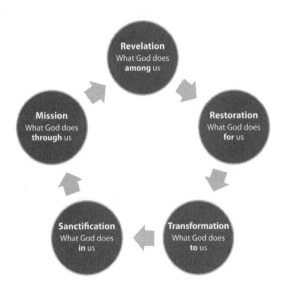

The saints of the past asserted frequently and forcefully that true depth is within reach, but we must want it more than life itself. I wrote this book so that we would *want* to want true depth more and more—enough to radically pursue it. Yet in our pursuit we must remember our dependence upon grace. Brother Lawrence reminded us: "The greater the perfection a soul seeks, the more dependent it is on grace, and the help of God is more necessary for it each moment for without it the soul can do nothing; the world, human nature and the devil together wage a war so fierce and so continual that without this actual help and this humble and necessary dependence, they will carry the soul away in spite of itself; this seems hard on human nature but grace makes it acceptable and a refuge."[1]

Brother Lawrence was convinced that sainthood, true depth, is attainable, but only by the grace of God. Again, God is the one who makes disciples.

Imagine a church full of deep disciples, disciples who dare to break free from the shallows of cultural churchianity to experience the depths of biblical Christianity. They are disciples who stop, look, and listen for the God who shows up and speaks up to reveal himself among us. They are enamored with the God of grace who provides restorative mulligans when we slice the ball of our lives into the woods. They are transformed when God does something extraordinary to them through the process of brokenness. They are disciples who experience a sanctifying work of God in them through the frustrating but formative local church. They are disciples who engage in mission by stepping into the tight and terrifying space between the bullied and the bullies, so God builds his kingdom through them. When I dream about disciples of depth, I can't contain my excitement. How about you? Let's become disciples of true depth because, by God's grace, we can.

SWIMMER'S PRAYER

Lord, we need you. Help us to see past the nose on our face to your powerful grace. Make us what you have determined we ought to be. Deepen our loving devotion to you so that we are more committed than ever to swim in deep waters. Keep reminding and convincing us that the most effective way for us to positively impact the world is to actually be the church. Make us one. Give us courage. Stretch our faith. Grant us depth. True depth. Amen.

NOTE

1. Brother Lawrence, *The Practice of the Presence of God*, trans. John J. Delaney (New York: Doubleday, 1977), 86.